William Faulkner

THE PROFILES IN LITERATURE SERIES

GENERAL EDITOR: B. C. SOUTHAM, M.A., B.LITT. (OXON.)
*Formerly Department of English, Westfield College,
University of London*

Volumes in this series include

William Faulkner

by Eric Mottram

Lecturer in American Literature
King's College, University of London

LONDON

ROUTLEDGE & KEGAN PAUL

First published 1971
by Routledge and Kegan Paul Ltd
Broadway House
68-74 Carter Lane
London, EC4V 5EL
Printed in Great Britain
by Northumberland Press Ltd
Gateshead 8
© Eric Mottram 1971
ISBN 0 7100 6988 x

The Profiles in Literature Series

This series is designed to provide the student of literature and the general reader with a brief and helpful introduc- tion to the major novelists and prose writers in English, American and foreign literature.

Each volume will provide an account of an individual author's writing career and works, through a series of care- fully chosen extracts illustrating the major aspects of the author's art. These extracts are accompanied by commen- tary and analysis, drawing attention to particular features of the style and treatment. There is no pretence, of course, that a study of extracts can give a sense of the works as a whole, but this selective approach enables the reader to focus his attention upon specific features, and to be in- formed in his approach by experienced critics and scholars who are contributing to the series.

The volumes will provide a particularly helpful and practical form of introduction to writers whose works are extensive or which present special problems for the modern reader, who can then proceed with a sense of his bearings and an informed eye for the writer's art.

An important feature of these books is the extensive re- ference list of the author's works and the descriptive list of the most useful biographies, commentaries and critical studies.

B.C.S.

Acknowledgments

The author and publisher wish to thank the Author's Literary Estate and Chatto & Windus Ltd for permission to use copyright material from: *The Sound and the Fury, As I Lay Dying, Absalom, Absalom, Go Down, Moses, The Hamlet* and *The Mansion.*

Contents

William Faulkner—his life and works

As the voluble lawyer Gavin Stevens remarks in *Requiem for a Nun*, 'the past is never dead. It's not even past'. If one single principle could be said to govern William Faulkner's sensibility, this would be it. His works, across more than forty years of creative life, constitute an imaginative recovery of a past which lives in the present and whose imagined, mythical power binds history into the future. Faulkner's onward going voice—and his prose is essentially oral and should ideally be read aloud with a persistent, yarning insistence—holds together the energy of events which continually threaten to refuse boundary and cause chaos. Faulkner is a virtuoso story-teller and this selection is designed to provide examples of his varied performance. No selection could possibly be more than minimally effective for the simple reason that his very manner demands that you hear him through, learn his immediate technique, and read again, relaxed into the characters and action which you have learned through his style. Beyond pleasures in his pyrotechnics, he demands that you take part in the origins of his energy and the effects of his fire and light in the human environment. But pleasure in Faulkner begins with his marvellous range of actions and characters, his delight in plots as involved and reflexive as life itself, and his continuous creation of a world spread through a career of over twenty-five books, between 1924 and 1962. William Faulkner is a writer of an originality and power barely equalled since Henry James and James Joyce.

But his moral vision of human life—in the South, in America, among human beings in the world—is particular and dogged: a dramatized, complex set of attitudes and feelings which emerge from the fact that, besides being a writer, Faulkner behaved as a landed gentleman in the rural South, a region neither racially nor socially egalitarian. Faulkner's South is a hierarchical society based on family, class, property, land and money, still vengefully smarting under the defeat of the Civil War and the apparent humiliations of the Reconstruction, and still only barely moving into industrial democratic America with painful slowness and resentment at the changes which are inevitable. Faulkner's affection of being not a writer but a farmer has its roots in a personal wariness before the chance of losing location, which is part of the conservatism of the region in which he was born and lived most of his life.

He is no more a lovable model for democracy than Shakespeare. His ability lies elsewhere, in an inventive language which articulates his imagination as it remembers or creates characters in action. We yield to the storyteller but discriminate carefully the morality of his opinions and world-view. In a period when the very word 'Negro' has been replaced by 'black' because 'Negro' is a white invention to stereotype darkly pigmented people so that they could be conveniently used as a cheap labour source and a sexually inferior group in the scale between men and animals, and in a time when the conflicts between

rural poor whites, small town bourgeois and political aristocracy bursts out of the television screens of the world,
Faulkner's attitudes cannot be simply accepted as the
idiosyncratic imaginings of an ineffectual novelist. His
opinions have the projective power of his genius and they
consolidate widely-held attitudes and feelings about men
and the land.

While it is treacherous to select from his career, it is
relatively easy to point to the peak of his creativity, between *The Sound and the Fury* in 1929 and *Go Down,
Moses* in 1942. The ten novels and close assemblages of
related stories during this period are a major achievement
in the history of fiction. Faulkner is inventing new post-
Joycean forms in which to involve the reader's sensibility,
the visual equivalent of the outpouring, onward going
voice we hear on the LP he made, reading passages from
As I Lay Dying, A Fable and *The Wild Palms,* and the
Nobel Prize address of 1950. Faulkner's prose styles and
plot structures are tense with his urgency to get down into
a stable form the sheer abundance of his imagined ver-
sion of Lafayette County, Mississippi, the geography,
society, history and hagiography of Yoknapatawpha
County. He transforms his home ground as Dickens
changed London or Milton imagined the maps and myths
of the Christian universe.

Faulkner's abundance is presented in broadly dramatic
chiaroscuro; the subtleties are mainly in the language
rather than in gradations of sensitivity and knowledge.
Thomas Sutpen dynastically married by the light of torches
held by his imported blacks; Joe Christmas circling to his
castration as a Negro by a proto-fascist incensed with a
righteousness now only too familiar in the world of the
Sixties; Lucas Beauchamp's proud neutralization of his
vulnerability as a Negro in order to survive as a basic
instance of dignity; the idiot Benjy Compson's discon-

3

tinuous memory as he inadvertently focuses the disintegration of his family; the boy Vardaman hearing his mother bubbling in her coffin and dreaming of her as a fish; the almost superhuman endurance of the Bundren family as they cross a torrential river with the mother's body; Ike McCaslin's initiation confrontation with buck, bear and serpent in the wilderness of primeval America; and the whole Snopes clan of grotesques warped into the shapes of Faulkner's apprehensive delineation of capitalist enterprise and the power of money freed from community obligation: these are high instances of his world of self-educating men and women—whites, blacks, Indians, and their inter-offspring in actions more than life-size. Their stature grows from Faulkner's insistence that they discover themselves and their world empirically, at first hand, with all the anguish and ridicule that may imply, since most of his characters are ignorant, ill-educated, non-urban, unsophisticated and remote from the inheritance of Renaissance, Enlightenment and the applied science and critical philosophy of the nineteenth century. Their heroic stances are achieved and their collapses are managed at their own expense of energy. It is as if they inherited, without resentment and indeed without knowledge, little or nothing of what Europe and the Europeanizing world of Boston and New York, and the universities, would call culture; and even in the French classicizing styled mansions of the Southern white rulers only the veneers of eighteenth-century gentility can form a light crust over the thrusting barbarism.

Faulkner applied his reading in Cervantes, Balzac, Dickens and Joyce to the job of presenting his imagination of a world not in their tradition, although it may be said that these great novelists, in common with many others, were not overly concerned with educated, enlightened people in a balanced society. Like them, Faulkner is an organizer of men and women in dilemmas for which they have inherited no assured solution; but an American and a Southerner would be more in a position to realize what such a proposition might entail. The gentlemanly 'Mr. Bill', as the less wealthy knew him, did not want to change his world; rather, he wished to recreate the pleasure he found in its joy and pain and in the complex of its relationships, so that it flooded his mind to the exclusion of any other scene. When he turned to the myth of war, salvation and mutiny in *A Fable*, the First World War became an extension of his vision of the South into a universalization which fatally lacked the visual and linguistic substance of Yoknapatawpha.

His style conveys his flooded sensibility. While we read him the oncoming flow of words, the loud cadences and paragraphic sentences, and pages without punctuation overwhelm the body with sensuous power. Faulkner's humour, like Mark Twain's, is usually in the service of an understanding of social corruption; the smarting ridicule and fear within *Huckleberry Finn* is present in Faulkner's analysis of greed and malign sexuality in the same scene as Twain's: the South. The difference is that Faulkner is rarely boisterous at the expense of the land-owning classes and old families, and his attitudes towards 'Negroes' cuts ambiguously into his broad humanism. There is a sentimentality in his allegiances to the Compsons and their black servant Dilsey which you will not find in *Life on the Mississippi* or *Pudd'nhead Wilson*. Part of the reason is that he valued loyalty above all other qualities, and loyalty is a personal action which may be offered to any cause, person, idea or region, without the discrimination of any other, impersonal, critical energy or sympathy.

In Japan in 1958 Faulkner noted the loyalty of a woman who served him; it is his single most powerful impression of that country, and completely characteristic of his aristocratic manners:

She calls me wise man and teacher, who am neither; when speaking of me to others: she is proud to have me for her client and, I hope, pleased that I try to deserve that pride and match with courtesy that loyalty. There is a lot of loose loyalty in this land. Even a little of it is too valuable to be ignored.

And he adds, comparing Japan with the South, 'nature is the same: only the economy is different'. From Faulkner's *Essays, Speeches and Public Letters*, especially in his fine essay in selective history, 'Mississippi', it is clear that his loyalty to the historical South within his mythical South is fundamental. Part of himself went into the making of Ike McCaslin, the last inheritor and relinquisher of white agrarian settlement in Yoknapatawpha, and Dilsey contains much of Caroline Barr, to whom *Go Down, Moses* is dedicated, and whose valedictory sermon he pronounced in honour of her devoted loyalty and endurance as the family servant. The other point of view is offered by the black American writer, Ralph Ellison, who remarked of this side of Faulkner: 'loyalty given where one's humanity is unrecognized seems a bit obscene'.

Faulkner's women remain, throughout his fiction, for the most part either broad symbols of loyalty or betrayers of loyalty; there is hardly a developed character among them, since even Dilsey, the black woman who holds together the decaying house of Compson in *The Sound and the Fury*, cannot be shown in other than a small area of housekeeping loyalty and revivalist Christianity. Nancy Mannigoe, another black servant, is hired by Temple Stevens, whose sexual ambivalence in *Sanctuary* is reconstituted in *Requiem for a Nun*, because she had been a prostitute and a drug addict, making her servitude an opportunity for redemption through loyalty. In *The Town* and several of his last works, Faulkner 'redeems' sensual women from what he thought of as sexual evils. But loyalty cannot be made a clear moral pivot for a fictional action, and Faulkner staked a great deal on this virtue. In fact, his South forms up as a community of loyalties and disloyalties. Even the aggressively opportunist Snopes clan sets up a counter-loyalty of egoism, rapacity and vain energy against the traditional community, challenging agrarian hierarchies of family, land and slaves or servants —among both whites and Indians—with greed and sexual coarseness which emerge as winning counter-energy, over-lapping only too obviously with the genteel masks of the established order.

Faulkner presents the Snopeses with his usual obsessive care but finally he can do no more than laugh uneasily at their grotesque nature. After all, misplaced loyalty has been a major curse in the twentieth century, and the gro-tesque has reached brutal power again and again; Chaplin's Hitler does not remove the tyrant of history. Faulkner's characters are grotesques warped by their societies' pres-sure; the classic example is Joe Christmas, a man who may be part black in some remote ancestry, shaped and alienated by the varieties of fanaticism which constitute the culture of *Light in August*. He is caught in a web of prejudice about race, colour, sex and religion, whose shaping weight hounds him, as he hounds himself, to a death which Faulk-ner offers as a brutal waste of blood and sexual energy. In doing so, as Cleanth Brooks reminds us in his study of the Yoknapatawpha books:

Faulkner has let us see our modern and complex problems mirrored in a simpler and more primitive world. *Light in August* is, in some respects, a bloody and violent pastoral.

The pace of his story-telling is the pace of a region

transmuted into such a simpler world. The very name of his invented county of Mississippi is a Choctaw Indian word meaning, as Faulkner said, 'water runs slow through flat land'. His pastoral has the slowness of apparent inevitability. It is that apparently fixed nature and fixed human nature which informs everything he writes. He charms the reader into a willing suspension of any belief in change or possible alternative world. His hostile environment is primeval and everlasting. The ledgers in which Ike McCaslin reads the web of his ancestry become the spatial history of the whole region and the larger context of human, Christianized history:

as the stereopticon condenses into one instantaneous field the myriad minutiae of its scope, so did that slight and rapid gesture [his cousin has just raised his hand] establish in the small cramped and cluttered room not only the ledgers but the whole plantation in its mazed and intricate entirety ... that whole edifice intricate and complex and founded upon injustice and erected by ruthless rapacity and carried on even yet with at times downright savagery not only to human beings but the valuable animals too, yet solvent and efficient and, more than that: not only still intact but enlarged, increased.

This passage from 'The Bear' in *Go Down, Moses* is the epitome of Faulkner's rigid and labyrinthine vision of life. His plot and his sentence are the logic of the desire implicit both here and in his statement to Malcolm Cowley:

I'm trying to say it all in one sentence, between one cap and one period. I'm still trying to put it all if possible on one pinhead.... Art is simpler than people think because there is so little to write about. All the moving things are eternal in man's history and have been written before.

The elaborate kinship systems within or between Faulk-

8

ner's families—Compson, Snopes, McCaslin, Sartoris, Sutpen—suggest a continuity which can only peter out when the dynastic energies are drained by the inroads of other systems of life which rely on the efficiency of machine technology and the amoral machinations of money to perpetuate their victories over people who once based their lives on the functions of soil, river and forest. Law, in the shape of curtailment of these energies and decays, is very nearly impotent within Faulkner's drama of men and women with fanatical loyalties.

Faulkner's work is complex but clear. The mass of exegesis which now surrounds and threatens to embed his work is largely unnecessarily intimidating to anyone first embarking on his journey out, into Yoknapatawpha. The feel of Faulkner's own excitement is quite unmistakable. His complexity of formal narratives can easily be learned, and his moral vision, whatever one may think of it, is not obscure. He is a novelist and not a philosopher. Towards the end of his life, while writer-in-residence at the University of Virginia, he said:

I read *Don Quixote* every year. I read the Old Testament. I read some of Dickens every year, and I've got a portable Shakespeare, one-volume Shakespeare, that I carry along with me. Conrad, *Moby-Dick*, Chekhov, *Madame Bovary*, some Balzac almost every year, Tolstoy ... Gogol. Most of the Frenchmen of the nineteenth century I read every year....

Faulkner clearly felt himself to be within the tradition of western fiction in themes and styles, and the Old Testament and Shakespeare certainly penetrates his rhetoric. But he counters this inheritance with the truth of his regionalism: 'I am not a writer', he told his Japanese audience, 'I am a peasant—even if I do write books and people read them'. His fiction rises between his sense of

9

belonging to a completed, closed land area, with its interlocking history of events, and his sensibility imbued with the great fiction of the west. Behind his constant and typically twentieth-century experimenting with style and plot lies a large working library in his rooms at Oxford, Mississippi, and Charlottesville, Virginia. His personal copy of Joyce's *Ulysses* is dated 1924, a sure sign of his awareness of his trade.

Towards the end of his life, Faulkner felt the need to stabilize the conflicts of his hostile environment, and *The Reivers* (1962) indicates at least what he intended. But he could do little for the Snopes intrusion. In 1959 he finished, as he said, 'a work conceived and begun in 1925'. The seed of *The Mansion*, the last of the Snopes series, began to grow in the twenty-eight-year old man's fantasies, shared with his old Oxford friend, Phil Stone—that their beloved state was being undermined by a class without conscience, yet born as if from the land itself, and their rapacity part of its rapacity. Early Snopes clan stories went into *The Hamlet* (1940), a work balancing humour with loathing for the breed, as a strategy for reducing their curse as much as possible. But the rise of the Snopeses, from barn-burning tenant farmers to Jefferson bankers (in *The Mansion*, Flem Snopes lives in the ante-bellum mansion of Major de Spain, the aristocratic hunter of 'The Bear') is as grandiose as the dynastic ascent of Thomas Sutpen in *Absalom, Absalom* (1936), and their fall as ignominiously plotted by the vengeful Faulkner. In *The Hamlet* Flem had married Eula Varner, the pregnant daughter of a local citizen of means; in *The Town* (1957) she fries steaks in his lunchroom and captivates the mayor of Jefferson, Major de Spain. Flem is rewarded by being made superintendent of the power-house and then vice-president of the Merchants and Farmers Bank. The Snopeses proliferate, stealing and swindling in a more obvious way than their traditional and self-styled betters. Flem becomes president of the bank founded by Colonel Sartoris, the epitome of Southern aristocracy (*Sartoris*, 1929), but Faulkner takes revenge on his centre of blatant rather than concealed capitalism through Mink Snopes, a murderer betrayed by his cousin in 1908 and out for retribution.

Faulkner has a nineteenth-century love of destiny programming, and dynastic retribution is his favourite device for showing pattern in human lives. He found the metamorphoses of time and selection quite as alluring as Darwin or Ibsen did. The last in the family usually embodies his sense of disaster, merited or ironical, or the sense of the dubious chances of change. Flem Snopes's step-daughter obtains Mink's pardon, after thirty-eight years, in the hope that he will avenge her mother Eula Snopes's suicide. Faulkner gives her more than most of his women but for some reason will not let her marry the lawyer Gavin Stevens, whom she loves. He gives her adventures in New York and a chance to educate Negroes, but the writing is not as strong here as it is for Mink Snopes, a man who *completes* a family destiny.

Faulkner's prose usually energizes particularly where the Mississippi soil, earth and river suggest the security of natural permanences (however turbulent, as they are in the convict sections of *The Wild Palms*), and where a man or a woman lives out a completeness of which the land is the inclusive instance. Mink Snopes is the only Snopes to have a sense of the soil, and this helps to excuse his murder of a rapacious banker relative. In *The Reivers* Faulkner relinquishes most of his brooding sense of entangled energies at the centre of his web of nature and human nature. His most powerful work revolves round some unspeakable disaster and amoral force which may be only partly intuited and partly discovered by language —some old curse, and aboriginal fate which simply being human on this earth entails. It comprises every effort towards humanistic community and easeful stability. But in this last story, Lucius Priest lucidly tells how, in fairy-tale style, the younger sons and servants triumph over ancient gloom. Through the retrospective and amusing narrative, Faulkner returns to that world of hunting camps, families, and confused black and white relationships magnificently delineated in *Go Down, Moses*. He returns, too, to his theme of the encroachment of machines into agrarian traditional society. But his tone and speed are equally relaxed. His child hero challenges authority (it is a recurrent theme of American fiction) as the untried focus of moral decisions between classes and races, and between money and honour. The villain, as in *Sanctuary*, is a sexually obsessed man without community values, a figure of impotence in many ways. Without yielding to the Snopeses, Faulkner is confident enough to allow the machine, a car, into the future of Yoknapatawpha, and to allow a Negro to win a defeat of his white bosses, even if he does not follow it up with any radical demands. *The Reivers* is a stabilizing comedy of the measure of peace Faulkner dreamed could be managed, without the intrusion of Northern reformist notions. The date is firmly 1905; part of the book appeared in *Esquire* magazine (just as many of his stories appeared in the *Saturday Evening Post*); it is a popular novel, sentimentally nostalgic and emotionally reassuring in a turbulent time. But the real time is that of the Greenville sit-ins for black power, against which nostalgia is impotent.

As Allen Tate once wrote of Faulkner: 'no European could have written his books'. But there is no question of provincial regionalism here. His craftsmanship has a universal validity. His American quality has to do with the heroic scale of that victimization and passivity which preoccupies the novelists of both Europe and America during the past two hundred years. In America, from Brockden Brown and Poe onwards, this legend says that society is the image of forces which operate in nature as dark energies which hit back at self-reliance. Human nature and the nature of the earth's landscape and seasons are a single structure, both beneficent and malign, but finally destructive, fickle and deathly. In Tate's words:

Faulkner is one of the great exemplars of the international school of fiction which for more than a century has reversed the Aristotelian doctrine that tragedy is an action, not a quality.

On the Greco-Trojan myth Faulkner imposes the myth of Americans—Southerners, Northerners, Indians, Negroes —and reverts to what he calls the Dark Diceman or the Player who invents the rules and governs the game of necessity which reduces men to parts of an action. The whole of the action they may only intuit, and late in their lives, if ever. American history and geography are re-structured as archaicizing myth with these epic proportions, as if Americans needed such reference for their justification and stability. Since slavery and the hubristic exploitation of the land are not exclusively American crimes, but international actions, Faulkner's profound core is international. Slavery and land exploitation without conscience are caused by and release the energies of men in endless charges so repetitive that they seem to be inevitable history. Life, Faulkner says in his *Paris Review* interview,

Life is motion, and motion is concerned with what makes man move—which is ambition, power, pleasure. What time a man can devote to morality, he must take by force from the motions of which he is part. He is compelled to make choices between good and evil sooner or later, because moral conscience demands that from him in order that he can live with himself tomorrow. His moral conscience is the curse he had to accept from the gods in order to gain from them the right to dream.

The Sound and the Fury (1929)

Since this novel is particularly spatial and reflexive in com-
position, and is built round complex space and time structures, it is almost impossible to make coherently self-
contained extracts from it. The Compson family, whom it
mostly concerns, is Faulkner's major instance of nostalgia,
impotence and decay among Southern families. As their
lineage peters out in idiocy, wild bids for sexual freedom
and obsessive gambling, so their energy is spent in eternal
return to an imaginary glorious past and the chance of
regaining strength in the future. The novel is a superbly
complex story of futility, with only the Negro servant
class able to endure as white power dwindles. The first
passages are written from the point of view of Benjy
Compson, youngest son of Jason and Caroline Compson,
an idiot through whose timeless perception the life of the
family is first presented. His sister Caddy, his Negro guar-
dians, his brothers Quentin and Jason, the pasture the
father sold to a golf club, and the sexual reason for his
final incarceration are fused into a continuous action within a representation of his consciousness.

In the second passages, Quentin Compson, the eldest son,

is moving towards his suicide, obsessed by time, the decline of his family, his sister's sexuality, the selling of Benjy's pasture so that he could go to Harvard. Shreve McCannon is his room-mate at college, the student to whom he tells the story of Thomas Sutpen in *Absalom, Absalom*.

Benjy's monologue is dated 7 April, 1928, and Quentin's to 2 June, 1910.

I

'Benjy,' she said. 'How did you slip out. Where's Versh.'
She put her arms around me and I hushed and held to her dress and tried to pull her away.
'Why, Benjy.' she said. 'What is it. T. P.' she called.
The one in the swing got up and came, and I cried and pulled Caddy's dress.
'Benjy.' Caddy said. 'It's just Charlie. Dont you know Charlie.'
'Where's his nigger.' Charlie said. 'What do they let him run around loose for.'
'Hush, Benjy.' Caddy said. 'Go away, Charlie. He doesn't like you.' Charlie went away and I hushed. I pulled at Caddy's dress.
'Why, Benjy.' Caddy said. 'Aren't you going to let me stay here and talk to Charlie awhile.'
'Call that nigger.' Charlie said. He came back. I cried louder and pulled at Caddy's dress.
'Go away, Charlie.' Caddy said. Charlie came and put his hand on Caddy and I cried more. I cried loud.
'No, no.' Caddy said. 'No. No.'
'He can't talk.' Charlie said. 'Caddy.'
'Are you crazy.' Caddy said. She began to breathe fast. 'He can see. Dont. Dont.' Caddy fought. They both breathed fast. 'Please. Please.' Caddy whispered.
'Send him away.' Charlie said.
'I will.' Caddy said. 'Let me go.'
'Will you send him away.' Charlie said.
'Yes.' Caddy said. 'Let me go.' Charlie went away.

'Hush.' Caddy said. 'He's gone.' I hushed. I could hear her and feel her chest going.

'I'll have to take him to the house.' she said. She took my hand. 'I'm coming.' she whispered.

'Wait.' Charlie said. 'Call the nigger.'

'No.' Caddy said. 'I'll come back. Come on, Benjy.'

'Caddy.' Charlie whispered, loud. We went on. 'You better come back. Are you coming back.' Caddy and I were running. 'Caddy.' Charlie said. We ran out into the moonlight, toward the kitchen.

'Caddy.' Charlie said.

Caddy and I ran. We ran up the kitchen steps, onto the porch, and Caddy knelt down in the dark and held me. I could hear her and feel her chest. 'I wont.' she said. 'I wont anymore, ever. Benjy. Benjy.' Then she was crying, and I cried, and we held each other. 'Hush.' she said. 'Hush. I wont anymore.' So I hushed and Caddy got up and we went into the kitchen and turned the light on and Caddy took the kitchen soap and washed her mouth at the sink, hard. Caddy smelled like trees.

I kept a telling you to stay away from there, Luster said. They sat up in the swing, quick. Quentin had her hands on her hair. He had a red tie.

You crazy old loon, Quentin said. I'm going to tell Dilsey about the way you let him follow everywhere I go. I'm going to make her whip you good.

'I couldn't stop him.' Luster said. 'Come on here, Benjy.'

'Yes you could.' Quentin said. 'You didn't try. You were both snooping around after me. Did Grandmother send you all out here to spy on me.' She jumped out of the swing. 'If you don't take him right away this minute and keep him away, I'm going to make Jason whip you.'

'I can't do nothing with him.' Luster said. 'You try it if you think you can.'

'Shut your mouth.' Quentin said. 'Are you going to get him away.'

'Ah, let him stay.' he said. He had a red tie. The sun was red on it. 'Look here, Jack.' He struck a match and put it in his mouth. Then he took the match out of his mouth. It was still burning. 'Want to try it.' he said. I went over there. 'Open your mouth.' he said. I opened my mouth. Quentin hit the match with her hand and it went away.

'Goddamn you.' Quentin said. 'Do you want to get him started. Dont you know he'll beller all day. I'm going to tell Dilsey on you.' She went away running.

'Here, kid.' he said. 'Hey. Come on back. I aint going to fool with him.'

Quentin ran on to the house. She went around the kitchen.

'You played hell then, Jack.' he said. 'Aint you.'

'He cant tell what you saying.' Luster said. 'He deef and dumb.'

'Is.' he said. 'How long's he been that way.'

'Been that way thirty-three years today.' Luster said. 'Born looney. Is you one of them show folks.'

'Why.' he said.

'I don't ricklick seeing you around here before.' Luster said.

'Well, what about it.' he said.

'Nothing.' Luster said. 'I going tonight.'

He looked at me.

'You aint the one can play a tune on that saw, is you.' Luster said.

'It'll cost you a quarter to find that out.' he said. He looked at me. 'Why dont they lock him up.' he said. 'What'd you bring him out here for.'

'You aint talking to me.' Luster said. 'I cant do nothing with him. I just come over here looking for a quarter I lost so I can go to the show tonight. Look like now I aint going to get to go.' Luster looked on the ground. 'You aint got no extra quarter, is you.' Luster said.

'No,' he said. 'I aint.'

'I reckon I just have to find that other one, then.' Luster said. He put his hand in his pocket. 'You dont want to buy no golf ball neither, does you.' Luster said.

'What kind of ball.' he said.

'Golf ball.' Luster said. 'I don't want but a quarter.'

'What for.' he said. 'What do I want with it.'

'I didn't think you did.' Luster said. 'Come on here, mulehead.' he said. 'Come on here and watch them knocking that ball. Here something you can play with along with that jimson weed.' Luster picked it up and gave it to me. It was bright.

'Where'd you get that.' he said. His tie was red in the sun, walking.

'Found it under this here bush.' Luster said. 'I thought for a minute it was that quarter I lost.'

He came and took it.

'Hush.' Luster said. 'He going to give it back when he done looking at it.'

'Agnes Mabel Becky.' he said. He looked toward the house.

'Hush.' Luster said. 'He fixing to give it back.'

He gave it to me and I hushed.

'Who come to see her last night.' he said.

'I dont know.' Luster said. 'They comes every night she can climb down that tree. I dont keep no track of them.'

'Damn if one of them didn't leave a track.' he said. He looked at the house. Then he went and lay down in the swing. 'Go away.' he said. 'Dont bother me.'

'Come on here.' Luster said. 'You done played hell now. Time Miss Quentin get done telling on you.'

We went to the fence and looked through the curling flower spaces. Luster hunted in the grass.

'I had it right here.' he said. I saw the flag flapping, and the sun slanting on the broad grass.

'They'll be some along soon.' Luster said. 'There some now, but they going away. Come on and help me look for it.'

We went along the fence.

'Hush.' Luster said. 'How can I make them come over here, if they aint coming. Wait. They'll be some in a minute. Look yonder. Here they come.'

I went along the fence, to the gate, where the girls

passed with their booksatchels. 'You, Benjy.' Luster said. 'Come back here.'

You cant do no good looking through the gate, T. P. said. Miss Caddy done gone long ways away. Done got married and left you. You cant do no good, holding to the gate and crying. She cant hear you.

What is it he wants, T. P. Mother said. Cant you play with him and keep him quiet.

He want to go down yonder and look through the gate, T. P. said.

Well, he cannot do it, Mother said. It's raining. You will just have to play with him and keep him quiet. You, Benjamin.

Aint nothing going to quiet him, T. P. said. He think if he down to the gate, Miss Caddy come back.

Nonsense, Mother said.

I could hear them talking. I went out the door and I couldn't hear them, and I went down to the gate, where the girls passed with their booksatchels. They looked at me, walking fast, with their heads turned. I tried to say, but they went on, and I went along the fence, trying to say, and they went faster. Then they were running and I came to the corner of the fence and I couldn't go any further, and I held to the fence, looking after them and trying to say.

'You, Benjy.' T. P. said. 'What you doing, slipping out. Dont you know Dilsey whip you.'

'You cant do no good, moaning and slobbering through the fence.' T. P. said. 'You done skeered them chillen. Look at them, walking on the other side of the street.'

How did he get out, Father said. Did you leave the gate unlatched when you came in, Jason.

Of course not, Jason said. Dont you know I've got better sense than to do that. Do you think I wanted anything like this to happen. This family is bad enough, God knows. I could have told you, all the time. I reckon you'll send him to Jackson, now. If Mrs Burgess dont shoot him first.

Hush, Father said.

I could have told you, all the time, Jason said.

It was open when I touched it, and I held to it in the twilight. I wasn't crying, and I tried to stop, watching the girls coming along in the twilight. I wasn't crying.

'There he is.'

They stopped.

'He cant get out. He wont hurt anybody, anyway. Come on.'

'I'm scared to. I'm scared. I'm going to cross the street.'

'He cant get out.'

I wasn't crying.

'Don't be a 'fraid cat. Come on.'

They came on in the twilight. I wasn't crying, and I held to the gate. They came slow.

'I'm scared.'

'He wont hurt you. I pass here every day. He just runs along the fence.'

They came on. I opened the gate and they stopped, turning. I was trying to say, and I caught her, trying to say, and she screamed and I was trying to say and trying and the bright shapes began to stop and I tried to get out. I tried to get it off my face, but the bright shapes were going again. They were going up the hill to where it fell away and I tried to cry. But when I breathed in, I couldn't breathe out again to cry, and I tried to keep from falling off the hill and I fell off the hill into the bright, whirling shapes.

II

I could smell the curves of the river beyond the dusk and I saw the last light supine and tranquil upon tide-flats like pieces of broken mirror, then beyond them lights began in the pale clear air, trembling a little like butter-flies hovering a long way off. Benjamin the child of. How he used to sit before that mirror. Refuge unfailing in which conflict tempered silenced reconciled. Benjamin the child of mine old age held hostage into Egypt. O Benjamin. Dilsey said it was because Mother was too proud for him. They come into white people's lives like that in sudden sharp black trickles that isolate white facts for an instant in unarguable truth like under a miscroscope; the rest of the time just voices that laugh when you see nothing to laugh at, tears when no reason for tears. They will bet on the odd or even number of mourners at a funeral. A brothel full of them in Memphis went into a religious trance ran naked into the street. It took three policemen to subdue one of them. Yes Jesus O good man Jesus O that good man.

The car stopped. I got out, with them looking at my eye. When the trolley came it was full. I stopped on the back platform.

'Seats up front,' the conductor said. I looked into the car. There were no seats on the left side.

'I'm not going far,' I said. 'I'll just stand here.'

We crossed the river. The bridge, that is, arching slow and high into space, between silence and nothingness where lights—yellow and red and green—trembled in the clear air, repeating themselves.

'Better go up front and get a seat,' the conductor said.

'I get off pretty soon,' I said. 'A couple of blocks.'

I got off before we reached the postoffice. They'd all be sitting around somewhere by now though, and then I was hearing my watch and I began to listen for the chimes and I touched Shreve's letter through my coat, the bitten shadows of the elms flowing upon my hand. And then as I turned into the quad the chimes did begin and I went on while the notes came up like ripples on a pool and passed me and went on, saying Quarter to what? All right. Quarter to what.

Our windows were dark. The entrance was empty. I walked close to the left wall when I entered, but it was empty: just the stairs curving up into shadows echoes of feet in the sad generations like light dust upon the shadows, my feet waking them like dust, lightly to settle again.

I could see the letter before I turned the light on, propped against a book on the table so I would see it. Calling him my husband. And then Spoade said they were

going somewhere, would not be back until late, and Mrs
Bland would need another cavalier. But I would have
seen him and he cannot get another car for an hour because after six oclock. I took out my watch and listened
to it clicking away, not knowing it couldnt even lie. Then
I laid it face up on the table and took Mrs Bland's letter
and tore it across and dropped the pieces into the waste
basket and took off my coat, vest, collar, tie and shirt.
The tie was spoiled too, but then niggers. Maybe a pattern
of blood he could call that the one Christ was wearing.
I found the gasoline in Shreve's room and spread the vest
on the table, where it would be flat, and opened the
gasoline.

*the first car in town a girl Girl that's what Jason
couldn't bear smell of gasoline making him sick then got
madder than ever because a girl Girl had no sister but
Benjamin Benjamin the child of my sorrowful if I'd just
had a mother so I could say Mother Mother* It took a lot
of gasoline, and then I couldnt tell if it was still the stain
or just the gasoline. It had started the cut to smarting
again so when I went to wash I hung the vest on a chair
and lowered the light cord so that the bulb would be
drying the splotch. I washed my face and hands, but even
then I could smell it within the soap stinging, constricting
the nostrils a little. Then I opened the bag and took the
shirt and collar and tie out and put the bloody ones in
and closed the bag, and dressed. While I was brushing
my hair the half hour went. But there was until the three
quarters anyway, except suppose *seeing on the rushing
darkness only his own face no broken feather unless two
of them but not two like that going to Boston the same
night then my face his face for an instant across the
crashing when out of darkness two lighted windows in
rigid fleeing crash gone his face and mine just I see saw
did I see not goodbye the marquee empty of eating the
road empty in darkness in silence the bridge arching into
silence darkness sleep the water peaceful and swift not
goodbye.*

I turned out the light and went into my bedroom, out

of the gasoline but I could still smell it. I stood at the window the curtains moved slow out of the darkness touching my face like someone breathing asleep, breathing slow into the darkness again, leaving the touch. *After they had gone up stairs Mother lay back in her chair, the camphor handkerchief to her mouth. Father hadn't moved he still sat beside her holding her hand the bellowing hammering away like no place for it in silence* When I was little there was a picture in one of our books, a dark place into which a single weak ray of light came slanting upon two faces lifted out of the shadow. *You know what I'd do if I were King?* she never was a queen or a fairy she was always a king or a giant or a general *I'd break that place open and drag them out and I'd whip them good* It was torn out, jagged out. I was glad. I'd have to turn back to it until the dungeon was Mother herself she and Father upward into weak light holding hands and us lost somewhere below even them without even a ray of light. Then the honeysuckle got into it. As soon as I turned off the light and tried to go to sleep it would begin to come into the room in waves building and building up until I would have to pant to get any air at all out of it until I would have to get up and feel my way like when I was a little boy *hands can see touching in the mind shaping unseen door Door now nothing hands can see* My nose could see gasoline, the vest on the table, the door. The corridor was still empty of all the feet in sad generations seeking water. *yet the eyes unseeing clenched like teeth not disbelieving doubting even the absence of pain shin ankle knee the long invisible flowing of the stair-railing where a misstep in the darkness filled with sleeping Mother Father Caddy Jason Maury door I am not afraid only Mother Father Caddy Jason Maury getting so far ahead sleeping I will sleep fast when I door Door door* It was empty too, the pipes, the porcelain, the stained quiet walls, the throne of contemplation. I had forgotten the glass, but I could *hands can see cooling fingers invisible swan-throat where less than Moses rod the glass touch tentative not to drumming lean cool throat drumming*

24

*cooling the metal the glass full overfull cooling the glass
the fingers flushing sleep leaving the taste of dampened
sleep in the long silence of the throat* I returned up the
corridor, waking the lost feet in whispering battalions in
the silence, into the gasoline, the watch telling its furious
lie on the dark table. Then the curtains breathing out of
the dark upon my face, leaving the breathing upon my
face. A quarter hour yet. And then I'll not be. The peacefullest words. Peacefullest words. *Non fui. Sum. Fui. Non
sum.* Somewhere I heard bells once. Mississippi or Massachusetts. I was. I am not. Massachusetts or Mississippi.
Shreve has a bottle in his trunk. *Aren't you even going
to open it* Mr and Mrs Jason Richmond Compson announce
the *Three times. Days. Aren't you even going to open it*
marriage of their daughter Candace *that liquor teaches
you to confuse the means with the end.* I am. Drink.
I was not. Let us sell Benjy's pasture so that Quentin
may go to Harvard and I may knock my bones together and together. I will be dead in. Was it one year
Caddy said. Shreve has a bottle in his trunk. Sir I will
not need Shreve's I have sold Benjy's pasture and I can
be dead in Harvard Caddy said in the caverns and the
grottoes of the sea tumbling peacefully to the wavering
tides because Harvard is such a fine sound forty acres
is no high price for a fine sound. A fine dead sound we
will swap Benjy's pasture for a fine dead sound. It will
last him a long time because he cannot hear it unless
he can smell it *as soon as she came in the door he began
to cry* I thought all the time it was just one of those
town squirts that Father was always teasing her about
until. I didn't notice him any more than any other stranger
drummer or what thought they were army shirts until
all of a sudden I knew he wasn't thinking of me at all
as a potential source of harm, but was thinking of her
when he looked at me was looking at me through her
like through a piece of coloured glass *why must you
meddle with me dont you know it wont do any good I
thought you'd have left that for Mother and Jason.*

did Mother set Jason to spy on you I wouldnt have.

Women only use other people's codes of honour it's because she loves Caddy staying downstairs even when she was sick so Father couldnt kid Uncle Maury before Jason Father said Uncle Maury was too poor a classicist to risk the blind immortal boy in person he should have chosen Jason because Jason would have made only the same kind of blunder Uncle Maury himself would have made not one to get him a black eye the Patterson boy was smaller than Jason too they sold the kites for a nickel apiece until the trouble over finances Jason got a new partner still smaller one small enough anyway because T. P. said Jason still treasurer but Father said why should Uncle Maury work if he father could support five or six niggers that did nothing at all but sit with their feet in the oven he certainly could board and lodge Uncle Maury now and then and lend him a little money who kept his Father's belief in the celestial derivation of his own species at such a fine heat then Mother would cry and say that Father believed his people were better than hers that he was ridiculing Uncle Maury to teach us the same thing she couldnt see that Father was teaching us that all men are just accumulations dolls stuffed with sawdust swept up from the trash heaps where all previous dolls had been thrown away the sawdust flowing from what wound in what side that not for me died not. It used to be I thought of death as a man something like Grandfather a friend of his a kind of private and particular friend like we used to think of Grandfather's desk not to touch it not even to talk loud in the room where it was I always thought of them as being together somewhere all the time waiting for old Colonel Sartoris to come down and sit with them waiting on a high place beyond cedar trees Colonel Sartoris was on a still higher place looking out across at something and they were waiting for him to get done looking at it and come down Grandfather wore his uniform and we could hear the murmur of their voices from beyond the cedars they were always talking and Grandfather was always right.

The three quarters began. The first note sounded,

measured and tranquil, serenely peremptory, emptying the unhurried silence for the next one and that's it if people could only change one another forever that way merge like a flame swirling up for an instant then blown cleanly out along the cool eternal dark instead of lying there trying not to think of the swing until all cedars came to have that vivid dead smell of perfume that Benjy hated so. Just by imagining the clump it seemed to me that I could hear whispers secret surges smell the beating of hot blood under wild unsecret flesh watching against red eyelids the swine untethered in pairs rushing coupled into the sea and he we must just stay awake and see evil done for a little while its not always and i it doesnt have to be even that long for a man of courage and he do you consider that courage and i yes sir dont you and he every man is the arbiter of his own virtues whether or not you consider it courageous is of more importance than the act itself than any act otherwise you could not be in earnest and i you dont believe i am serious and he i think you are too serious to give me any cause for alarm you wouldnt have felt driven to the expedient of telling me you have committed incest otherwise and i i wasnt lying i wasnt lying and he you wanted to sub-limate a piece of natural human folly into a horror and then exorcise it with truth and i it was to isolate her out of the loud world so that it would have to flee us of necessity and then the sound of it would be as though it had never been and he did you try to make her do it and i i was afraid to i was afraid she might and then it wouldnt have done any good but if i could tell you we did it would have been so and then the others wouldnt be so and then the world would roar away and he and now this other you are not lying now either but you are still blind to what is in yourself to that part of general truth the sequence of natural events and their causes which shadows every mans brow even benjys you are not thinking of finitude you are contemplating an apotheosis in which a temporary state of mind will become sym-metrical above the flesh and aware both of itself and of

27

the flesh it will not quite discard you will not even be dead and i temporary and he you cannot bear to think that someday it will no longer hurt you like this now were getting at it you seem to regard it merely as an experience that will whiten your hair overnight so to speak without altering your appearance at all you wont do it under these conditions it will be a gamble and the strange thing is that man who is conceived by accident and whose every breath is a fresh cast with dice already loaded against him will not face that final main which he knows before hand he has assuredly to face without essaying expedients ranging all the way from violence to petty chicanery that would not deceive a child until someday in very disgust he risks everything on a single blind turn of a card no man ever does that under the first fury of despair or remorse or bereavement he does it only when he has realised that even the despair or remorse or bereavement is not particularly important to the dark diceman and i temporary and he it is hard believing to think that a love or a sorrow is a bond purchased without design and which matures willynilly and is recalled without warning to be replaced by whatever issue the gods happen to be floating at the time no you will not do that until you come to believe that even she was not quite worth despair perhaps and i i will never do that nobody knows what i know and he i think youd better go on up to cambridge right away you might go up into maine for a month you can afford it if you are careful it might be a good thing watching pennies has healed more scars than jesus and i suppose i realise what you believe i will realise up there next week or next month and he then you will remember that for you to go to harvard has been your mothers dream since you were born and no compson has ever disappointed a lady and i temporary it will be better for me for all of us and he every man is the arbiter of his own virtues but let no man prescribe for another mans wellbeing and i temporary and he was the saddest word of all there is nothing else in the world its not despair until time its not even time until it was

The last note sounded. At last it stopped vibrating and the darkness was still again. I entered the sitting room and turned on the light. I put my vest on. The gasoline was faint now, barely noticeable, and in the mirror the stain didnt show. Not like my eye did, anyway. I put on my coat. Shreve's letter crackled through the cloth and I took it out and examined the address, and put it in my side pocket. Then I carried the watch into Shreve's room and put it in his drawer and went to my room and got a fresh handkerchief and went to the door and put my hand on the light switch.

As I Lay Dying (1930)

In his *Paris Review* interview Faulkner spoke of his fifth novel in a way which shows clearly the part experimental form played in his career:

Sometimes technique charges in and takes command of the dream before the writer himself can get his hands on it.... This happened with *As I Lay Dying* ... I simply imagined a group of people and subjected them to the simple universal catastrophes, which are flood and fire, with a simple natural motive to give direction to their progress.

The technique is fifty-nine interior monologues by fifteen characters, centred on one long section by Addie Bundren, the mother whose dead body her family is taking, at her request, to burial in Jefferson—Faulkner's 'natural motive'. Nineteen of the monologues are by Darl, the son cursed with articulation and self-consciousness; his rival is Jewel, the natural son of Addie and Preacher Whitfield, a man of passionate vitality which finds completion in horses and love for his mother.

The selected passage describes catastrophe by flood, as

the family reach the torrential river with Addie's coffin. Faulkner is writing heroically not of Indians, Negroes or elitist whites, but the farming and relatively poor families of Yoknapatawpha. Out of their unsophisticated rural lives he creates this epic pastoral of endurance :

... the thesis which I'm always hammering at: that man is indestructible because of his simple will to freedom....

Of the other characters here, Vardaman is the youngest son, who associates his mother with a fish, and bores holes in her coffin to let her breathe; Tull is a closely observing neighbour; and Cash is the eldest son, a carpenter who makes the coffin.

Darl

Before us the thick dark current runs. It talks up to us in a murmur become ceaseless and myriad, the yellow surface dimpled monstrously into fading swirls travelling along the surface for an instant, silent, impermanent and profoundly significant, as though just beneath the surface something huge and alive waked for a moment of lazy alertness out of and into light slumber again.

It clucks and murmurs among the spokes and about the mules' knees, yellow, scummed with flotsam and with thick soiled gouts of foam as though it had sweat, lathering, like a driven horse. Through the undergrowth it goes with a plaintive sound, a musing sound; in it the unwinded cane and saplings lean as before a little gale, swaying without reflections as though suspended on invisible wires from the branches overhead. Above the ceaseless surface they stand—trees, cane, vines—rootless, severed from the earth, spectral above a scene of immense yet circumscribed desolation filled with the voice of the waste and mournful water.

Cash and I sit in the wagon; Jewel sits the horse at

AS I LAY DYING (1930)

the off rear-wheel. The horse is trembling, its eye rolling
wild and baby-blue in its long pink face, its breathing
stertorous like groaning. He sits erect, poised, looking
quietly and steadily and quickly this way and that, his
face calm, a little pale, alert. Cash's face is also gravely
composed; he and I look at one another with long prob-
ing looks, looks that plunge unimpeded through one another's eyes and into the ultimate secret place where for
an instant Cash and Darl crouch flagrant and unabashed
in all the old terror and the old foreboding, alert and
secret and without shame. When we speak our voices are
quiet, detached.

'I reckon we're still in the road, all right.'

'Tull taken and cut them two big whiteoaks. I heard
tell how at high water in the old days they used to line
up the ford by them trees.'

'I reckon he did that two years ago when he was
logging down here. I reckon he never thought that anybody would ever use this ford again.'

'I reckon not. Yes, it must have been then. He cut a
sight of timber outen here then. Payed off that mortgage
with it, I hear tell.'

'Yes. Yes, I reckon so. I reckon Vernon could have done
that.'

'That's a fact. Most folks that logs in this here country,
they need a durn good farm to support the sawmill. Or
maybe a store. But I reckon Vernon could.'

'I reckon so. He's a sight.'

'Ay. Vernon is. Yes, it must still be here. He never
would have got that timber out of here if he hadn't
cleaned out that old road. I reckon we are still on it.'
He looks about quietly, at the position of the trees, leaning this way and that, looking back along the floorless
road shaped vaguely high in air by the position of the
lopped and felled trees, as if the road too had been soaked
free of earth and floated upward, to leave in its spectral
tracing a monument to a still more profound desolation
than this above which we now sit, talking quietly of old
security and old trivial things. Jewel looks at him, then

at me, then his face turns in that quiet, constant questing about the scene, the horse trembling quietly and steadily between his knees.

'He could go on ahead slow and sort of feel it out,' I say.

'Yes,' Cash says, not looking at me. His face is in profile as he looks forward where Jewel has moved on ahead.

'He can't miss the river,' I say. 'He couldn't miss seeing it fifty yards ahead.'

Cash does not look at me, his face in profile. 'If I'd just suspicioned it, I could 'a' come down last week and taken a sight on it.'

'The bridge was up then,' I say. He does not look at me. 'Whitfield crossed it a-horse-back.'

Jewel looks at us again, his expression sober and alert and subdued. His voice is quiet. 'What you want me to do?'

'I ought to come down last week and taken a sight on it,' Cash says.

'We couldn't have known,' I say. 'There wasn't any way for us to know.'

'I'll ride on ahead,' Jewel says. 'You can follow where I am.' He lifts the horse. It shrinks, bowed; he leans to it, speaking to it, lifting it forward almost bodily, it setting its feet down with gingerly splashings, trembling, breathing harshly. He speaks to it, murmurs to it. 'Go on,' he says. 'I ain't going to let nothing hurt you. Go on, now.'

'Jewel,' Cash says. Jewel does not look back. He lifts the horse on.

'He can swim,' I say. 'If he'll just give the horse time, anyhow ...' When he was born, he had a bad time of it. Ma would sit in the lamplight, holding him on a pillow on her lap. We would wake and find her so. There would be no sound from them.

'That pillow was longer than him,' Cash says. He is leaning a little forward. 'I ought to come down last week and sighted. I ought to done it.'

'That's right,' I say. 'Neither his feet nor his head would reach the end of it. You couldn't have known,' I say.

'I ought to done it,' he says. He lifts the reins. The mules move, into the traces; the wheels murmur alive in the water. He looks back and down at Addie. 'It aint on a balance,' he says.

At last the trees open; against the open river Jewel sits the horse, half turned, it belly deep now. Across the river we can see Vernon and pa and Vardaman and Dewey Dell. Vernon is waving at us, waving us further downstream.

'We are too high up,' Cash says. Vernon is shouting too, but we cannot make out what he says for the noise of the water. It runs steady and deep now, unbroken, without a sense of motion until a log comes along, turning slowly. 'Watch it,' Cash says. We watch it and see it falter and hang for a moment, the current building up behind it in a thick wave, submerging it for an instant before it shoots up and tumbles on.

'There it is,' I say.

'Ay,' Cash says. 'It's there.' We look at Vernon again. He is now flapping his arms up and down. We move on downstream, slowly and carefully, watching Vernon. He drops his hands. 'This is the place,' Cash says.

'Well, goddamn it, lets get across, then,' Jewel says. He moves the horse on.

'You wait,' Cash says. Jewel stops again.

'Well, by God—' he says. Cash looks at the water, then he looks back at Addie. 'It ain't on a balance,' he says.

'Then go on back to the goddamn bridge and walk across,' Jewel says. 'You and Darl both. Let me on that wagon.'

Cash does not pay him any attention. 'It ain't on a balance,' he says. 'Yes, sir. We got to watch it.'

'Watch it, hell,' Jewel says. 'You get out of that wagon and let me have it. By God, if you're afraid to drive it over ...' His eyes are pale as two bleached chips in his face. Cash is looking at him.

'We'll get it over,' he says. 'I tell you what you do. You ride on back and walk across the bridge and come down

the other bank and meet us with the rope. Vernon'll take
your horse home with him and keep it till we get back.'

'You go to hell,' Jewel says.

'You take the rope and come down the bank and be
ready with it,' Cash says. 'Three can't do no more than
two can—one to drive and one to steady it.'

'Goddamn you,' Jewel says.

'Let Jewel take the end of the rope and cross upstream
of us and brace it,' I say. 'Will you do that, Jewel?'

Jewel watches me, hard. He looks quick at Cash, then
back at me, his eyes alert and hard. 'I don't give a damn.
Just so we do something. Setting here, not lifting a goddamn hand . . .'

'Let's do that, Cash,' I say.

'I reckon we'll have to,' Cash says.

The river itself is not a hundred yards across, and pa
and Vernon and Vardaman and Dewey Dell are the only
things in sight not of that single monotony of desolation
leaning with that terrific quality a little from right to
left, as though we had reached the place where the motion
of the wasted world accelerates just before the final preci-
pice. Yet they appear dwarfed. It is as though the space
between us were time: an irrevocable quality. It is as
though time, no longer running straight before us in a
diminishing line, now runs parallel between us like a
looping string, the distance being the doubling accretion
of the thread and not the interval between. The mules
stand, their forequarters already sloped a little, their
rumps high. They too are breathing now with a deep
groaning sound; looking back once, their gaze sweeps
across us with in their eyes a wild, sad, profound and
despairing quality as though they had already seen in the
thick water the shape of the disaster which they could
not speak and we could not see.

Cash turns back into the wagon. He lays his hands flat
on Addie, rocking her a little. His face is calm, down-
sloped, calculant, concerned. He lifts his box of tools and
wedges it forward under the seat; together we shove Addie
forward, wedging her between the tools and the wagon-

bed. Then he looks at me.

'No,' I say. 'I reckon I'll stay. Might take both of us.'

From the tool-box he takes his coiled rope and carries the end twice around the seat stanchion and passes the end to me without tying it. The other end he pays out to Jewel, who takes a turn about his saddle-horn.

He must force the horse down into the current. It moves, high-kneed, arch-necked, boring and chafing. Jewel sits lightly forward, his knees lifted a little; again his swift alert calm gaze sweeps upon us and on. He lowers the horse into the stream, speaking to it in a soothing murmur. The horse slips, goes under to the saddle, surges to its feet again, the current building up against Jewel's thighs.

'Watch yourself,' Cash says.

'I'm on it now,' Jewel says. 'You can come ahead now.'

Cash takes the reins and lowers the team carefully and skilfully into the stream.

I felt the current take us and I knew we were on the ford by that reason, since it was only by means of that slipping contact that we could tell that we were in motion at all. What had once been a flat surface was now a succession of troughs and hillocks lifting and falling about us, shoving at us, teasing at us with light lazy touches in the vain instants of solidity underfoot. Cash looked back at me, and then I knew that we were gone. But I did not realize the reason for the rope until I saw the log. It surged up out of the water and stood for an instant upright upon that surging and heaving desolation like Christ. Get out and let the current take you down to the bend, Cash said. You can make it all right. No, I said, I'd get just as wet that way as this.

The log appears suddenly between two hills, as if it had rocketed suddenly from the bottom of the river. Upon the end of it a long gout of foam hangs like the beard of an old man or a goat. When Cash speaks to me I know that he has been watching it all the time, watching it and watching Jewel ten feet ahead of us. 'Let the rope go,' he says. With his other hand he reaches down and reeves the two turns from the stanchion. 'Ride on, Jewel,' he says; 'see if you can pull us ahead of the log.'

Jewel shouts at the horse; again he appears to lift it bodily between his knees. He is just above the top of the ford and the horse has a purchase of some sort for it surges forward, shining wetly half out of water, crashing on in a succession of lunges. It moves unbelievably fast; by that token Jewel realizes at last that the rope is free, for I can see him sawing back on the reins, his head turned, as the log rears in a long sluggish lunge between us bearing down upon the team. They see it too; for a moment they also shine black out of water. Then the downstream one vanishes, dragging the other with him; the wagon sheers crosswise, poised on the crest of the ford as the log strikes it, tilting it up and on. Cash is half turned, the reins running taut from his hand and disappearing into the water, the other hand reached back upon Addie, holding her jammed over against the high side of the wagon. 'Jump clear,' he says quietly. 'Stay away from the team and don't try to fight it. It'll swing you into the bend all right.'

'You come too,' I say. Vernon and Vardaman are running along the bank, pa and Dewey Dell stand watching us, Dewey Dell with the basket and the package in her arms. Jewel is trying to fight the horse back. The head of one mule appears, its eyes wide; it looks back at us for an instant, making a sound almost human. The head vanishes again.

'Back, Jewel,' Cash shouts. 'Back, Jewel.' For another instant I see him leaning to the tilting wagon, his arm braced back against Addie and his tools; I see the bearded head of the rearing log strike up again, and beyond it Jewel holding the horse upreared, its head wrenched around, hammering its head with his fist. I jump from the wagon on the downstream side. Between two hills I see the mules once more. They roll up out of the water in succession, turning completely over, their legs stiffly extended as when they had lost contact with the earth.

Vardaman

Cash tried but she fell off and Darl jumped going under he went under and Cash hollering to catch her and I hollering running and hollering and Dewey Dell hollering at me Vardaman you vardaman you vardaman and Vernon passed me because he was seeing her come up and she jumped into the water again and Darl hadn't caught her yet.

He came up to see and I hollering catch her Darl catch her and he didn't come back because she was too heavy he had to go on catching at her and I hollering catch her darl catch her darl because in the water she could go faster than a man and Darl had to grabble for her so I knew he could catch her because he is the best grabbler even with the mules in the way again they dived up rolling their feet stiff rolling down again and their backs up now and Darl had to again because in the water she could go faster than a man or a woman and I passed Vernon and he wouldn't get in the water and help Darl he would grabble for her with Darl but he wouldn't help.

The mules dived up again diving their legs stiff their stiff legs rolling slow and then Darl again and I hollering catch her darl catch her head her into the bank darl and Vernon wouldn't help and then Darl dodged past the mules where he could he had her under the water coming in to the bank coming in slow because in the water she fought to stay under the water but Darl is strong and he was coming in slow and so I knew he had her because he came slow and I ran down into the water to help and I couldn't stop hollering because Darl was strong and steady holding her under the water even if she did fight he would not let her go he was seeing me and he would hold her and it was all right now it was all right now it was all right.

Then he comes up out of the water. He comes a long way up slow before his hands do but he's got to have her got to so I can bear it. Then his hands come up and

*all of him above the water. I can't stop. I have not got
time to try. I will try to when I can but his hands came
empty out of the water emptying the water emptying
away.*

'Where is ma, Darl?' I said. 'You never got her. You
knew she is a fish but you let her get away. You never
got her. Darl. Darl. Darl.' I began to run along the bank,
watching the mules dive up slow again and then down
again.

Tull

When I told Cora how Darl jumped out of the wagon and
left Cash sitting there trying to save it and the wagon turning over, and Jewel that was almost to the bank fighting
that horse back where it had more sense than to go, she
says 'And you're one of the folk that says Darl is the queer
one, the one that ain't bright, and him the only one of them
that had sense enough to get off that wagon. I notice Anse
was too smart to been on it a-tall.'

'He couldn't 'a' done no good, if he'd been there,' I
said. 'They was going about it right and they would
have made it if it hadn't a-been for that log.'

'Log, fiddlesticks,' Cora said. 'It was the hand of God.'

'Then how can you say it was foolish?' I said. 'Nobody
can't guard against the hand of God. It would be sacri-
lege to try to.'

'Then why dare it?' Cora says. 'Tell me that.'

'Anse didn't,' I said. 'That's just what you faulted him
for.'

'His place was there,' Cora said. 'If he had been a man,
he would 'a' been there instead of making his sons do
what he dursn't.'

'I don't know what you want, then,' I said. 'One breath
you say they was daring the hand of God to try it, and the
next breath you jump on Anse because he wasn't with
them.' Then she begun to sing again, working at the wash-
tub, with that singing look in her face like she had done

39

give up folks and all their foolishness and had done went on ahead of them, marching up the sky, singing.

The wagon hung for a long time while the current built up under it, shoving it off, and Cash leaning more and more, trying to keep the coffin braced so it wouldn't slip down and finish tilting the wagon over. Soon as the wagon got tilted good, to where the current could finish it, the log went on. It headed around the wagon and went on good as a swimming man could have done. It was like it had been sent there to do a job and done it and went on.

When the mules finally kicked loose, it looked for a minute like maybe Cash would get the wagon back. It looked like him and the wagon wasn't moving at all, and just Jewel fighting that horse back to the wagon. Then that boy passed me, running and hollering at Darl and the gal trying to catch him, and then I see the mules come rolling slow up out of the water, their legs spraddled stiff like they had balked upside down, and roll on into the water again.

Then the wagon tilted over and then it and Jewel and the horse was all mixed up together. Cash went outen sight, still holding the coffin braced, and then I couldn't tell anything for the horse lunging and splashing. I thought that Cash had give up then and was swimming for it and I was yelling at Jewel to come on back and then all of a sudden him and the horse went under too and I thought they was all going. I knew that the horse had got dragged off the ford too, and with that wild drowning horse and that wagon and that loose box, it was going to be pretty bad, and there I was, standing knee deep in the water, yelling at Anse behind me: 'See what you done now. See what you done now?'

The horse come up again. It was headed for the bank now, throwing its head up, and then I saw one of them holding to the saddle on the downstream side, so I started running along the bank, trying to catch sight of Cash because he couldn't swim, yelling at Jewel where Cash was like a durn fool, bad as that boy that was on down the bank still hollering at Darl.

So I went down into the water so I could still keep some kind of grip in the mud, when I saw Jewel. He was middle deep, so I knew he was on the ford, anyway, leaning hard upstream, and then I see the rope and then I see the water building up where he was holding the wagon snubbed just below the ford.

So it was Cash holding to the horse when it come splashing and scrambling up the bank, moaning and groaning like a natural man. When I come to it it was just kicking Cash loose from his holt on the saddle. His face turned up a second when he was sliding back into the water. It was grey, with his eyes closed and a long swipe of mud across his face. Then he let go and turned over in the water. He looked just like an old bundle of clothes kind of washing up and down against the bank. He looked like he was laying there in the water on his face, rocking up and down a little, looking at something on the bottom.

We could watch the rope cutting down into the water, and we could feel the weight of the wagon kind of blump and lunge lazy like, like it just as soon as not, and that rope cutting down into the water hard as a iron bar. We could hear the water hissing on it like it was red hot. Like it was a straight iron bar stuck into the bottom and us holding the end of it, and the wagon lazing up and down, kind of pushing and prodding at us like it had come around and got behind us, lazy like, like it just as soon as not when it made up its mind. There was a shoat come by, blowed up like a balloon: one of them spotted shoats of Lon Quick's. It bumped again the rope like it was a iron bar and bumped off and went on, and us watching that rope slanting down into the water. We watched it.

Darl

Cash lies on his back on the earth, his head raised on a rolled garment. His eyes are closed, his face is grey, his hair plastered in a smooth smear across his forehead as though done with a paint-brush. His face appears sunken a little, sagging from the bony ridges of eye-sockets, nose, gums, as though the wetting had slacked the firmness which had held the skin full; his teeth, set in pale gums, are parted a little as if he had been laughing quietly. He lies pole-thin in his wet clothes, a little pool of vomit at his head and a thread of it running from the corner of his mouth and down his cheek where he couldn't turn his head quick or far enough, until Dewey Dell stoops and wipes it away with the hem of her dress.

Jewel approaches. He has the plane. 'Vernon just found the square,' he says. He looks down at Cash, dripping too. 'And he ain't talked none yet?'

'He had his saw and hammer and chalk-line and rule,' I say. 'I know that.'

Jewel lays the square down. Pa watches him. 'They can't be far away,' pa says. 'It all went together. Was there ere a such misfortunate man.'

Jewel does not look at pa. 'You better call Vardaman back here,' he says. He looks at Cash. Then he turns and goes away. 'Get him to talk soon as he can,' he says, 'so he can tell us what else there was.'

We return to the river. The wagon is hauled clear, the wheels chocked carefully: we all helped; it is as though upon the shabby, familiar, inert shape of the wagon there lingered somehow, latent yet still immediate, that violence which had slain the mules that drew it not an hour since) above the edge of the flood. In the wagon bed it lies profoundly, the long pale planks hushed a little with wetting yet still yellow, like gold seen through water, save for two long muddy smears. We pass it and go on to the bank.

One end of the rope is made fast to a tree. At the edge of the stream, knee-deep, Vardaman stands, bent forward a little, watching Vernon with rapt absorption. He has stopped yelling and he is wet to the armpits. Vernon is at the other end of the rope, shoulder-deep in the river, looking back at Vardaman. 'Further back than that,' he says. 'You git back by the tree and hold the rope for me, so it can't slip.'

Vardaman backs along the rope, to the tree, moving blindly, watching Vernon. When we come up he looks at us once, his eyes round and a little dazed. Then he looks at Vernon again in that posture of rapt alertness.

'I got the hammer too,' Vernon says. 'Looks like we ought to done already got that chalk-line. It ought to floated.'

'Floated clean away,' Jewel says. 'We won't get it. We ought to find the saw, though.'

'I reckon so,' Vernon says. He looks at the water. 'That chalk-line, too. What else did he have?'

'He ain't talked yet,' Jewel says, entering the water. He looks back at me. 'You go back and get him roused up to talk,' he says.

'Pa's there,' I say. I follow Jewel into the water, along the rope. It feels alive in my hand, bellied faintly in a prolonged and resonant arc. Vernon is watching me.

'You better go,' he says. 'You better be there.'

'Let's see what else we can get before it washes on down,' I say.

We hold to the rope, the current curling and dimpling about our shoulders. But beneath that false blandness the true force of it leans against us lazily. I had not thought that water in July could be so cold. It is like hands moulding and prodding at the very bones. Vernon is still looking back towards the bank.

'Reckon it'll hold us all?' he says. We too look back, following the rigid bar of the rope as it rises from the water to the tree and Vardaman crouched a little beside it, watching us. 'Wish my mule wouldn't strike out for home,' Vernon says.

'Come on,' Jewel says. 'Let's get outen here.'

We submerge in turn, holding to the rope, being clutched by one another while the cold wall of the water sucks the slanting mud backward and upstream from beneath our feet and we are suspended so, groping along the cold bottom. Even the mud there is not still. It has a chill, scouring quality, as though the earth under us were in motion too. We touch and fumble at one another's extended arms, letting ourselves go cautiously against the rope; or, erect in turn, watch the water suck and boil where one of the other two gropes beneath the surface. Pa has come down to the shore, watching us.

Vernon comes up, streaming, his face sloped down into his pursed blowing mouth. His mouth is bluish, like a circle of weathered rubber. He has the rule.

'He'll be glad of that,' I say. 'It's right new. He bought it just last month out of the catalogue.'

'If we just knowed for sho what else,' Vernon says, looking over his shoulder and then turning to face where Jewel had disappeared. 'Didn't he go down 'fore me?' Vernon says.

'I don't know,' I say. 'I think so. Yes, Yes, he did.'

We watch the thick curling surface, streaming away from us in slow whorls.

'Give him a pull on the rope,' Vernon says.

'He's on your end of it,' I say.

'Ain't nobody on my end of it,' he says.

'Pull it in,' I say. But he has already done that, holding the end above the water; and then we see Jewel. He is ten yards away; he comes up, blowing, and looks at us, tossing his long hair back with a jerk of his head, then he looks towards the bank; we can see him filling his lungs.

'Jewel,' Vernon says, not loud, but his voice going full and clear along the water, peremptory yet tactful. 'It'll be back here. Better come back.'

Jewel dives again. We stand there, leaning back against the current, watching the water where he disappeared, holding the dead rope between us like two men holding the nozzle of a fire-hose, waiting for the water. Suddenly Dewey Dell is behind us in the water. 'You make him come back,' she says. 'Jewel!' she says. He comes up again, tossing his hair back from his eyes. He is swimming now, toward the bank, the current sweeping him downstream quartering. 'You, Jewel!' Dewey Dell says. We stand holding the rope and see him gain the bank and climb out. As he rises from the water, he stoops and picks up something. He comes back along the bank. He has found the chalk-line. He comes opposite us and stands there, looking about as if he were seeking something. Pa goes on down the bank. He is going back to look at the mules again where their round bellies float and rub quietly together in the slack water within the bend.

'What did you do with the hammer, Vernon?' Jewel says.

'I give it to him,' Vernon says, jerking his head at Vardaman. Vardaman is looking after pa. Then he looks at Jewel. 'With the square.' Vernon is watching Jewel. He moves towards the bank, passing Dewey Dell and me.

'You can get out of here,' I say. She says nothing, looking at Jewel and Vernon.

'Where's the hammer?' Jewel says. Vardaman scuttles up the bank and fetches it.

'It's heavier than the saw,' Vernon says. Jewel is tying the end of the chalk-line about the hammer shaft.

'Hammer's got the most wood in it,' Jewel says. He and Vernon face one another, watching Jewel's hands.

'And flatter, too,' Vernon says. 'It'd float three to one, almost. Try the plane.'

Jewel looks at Vernon. Vernon is tall, too; long and lean, eye to eye they stand in their close wet clothes. Lon Quick could look even at a cloudy sky and tell the time to ten minutes. Big Lon I mean, not little Lon.

'Why don't you get out of the water?' I say.

'It won't float like a saw,' Jewel says.

'It'll float nigher to a saw than a hammer will,' Vernon says.

'Bet you,' Jewel says.

'I won't bet,' Vernon says.

They stand there, watching Jewel's still hands.

'Hell,' Jewel says. 'Get the plane, then.'

So they get the plane and tie it to the chalk-line and enter the water again. Pa comes back along the bank. He stops for a while and looks at us, hunched, mournful, like a failing steer or an old tall bird.

Vernon and Jewel return, leaning against the current.

45

'Get out of the way,' Jewel says to Dewey Dell. 'Get out of the water.'

She crowds against me a little so they can pass, Jewel holding the plane high as though it were perishable, the blue string trailing back over his shoulder. They pass us and stop; they fall to arguing quietly about just where the wagon went over.

'Darl ought to know,' Vernon says. They look at me.

'I don't know,' I says. 'I wasn't there that long.'

'Hell,' Jewel says. They move on, gingerly, leaning against the current, reading the ford with their feet.

'Have you got a holt of the rope?' Vernon says. Jewel does not answer. He glances back at the shore, calculant, then at the water. He flings the plane outward, letting the string run through his fingers, his fingers turning blue where it runs over them. When the line stops, he hands it back to Vernon.

'Better let me go this time,' Vernon says. Again Jewel does not answer, we watch him duck beneath the surface.

'Jewel,' Dewey Dell whimpers.

'It ain't so deep there,' Vernon says. He does not look back. He is watching the water where Jewel went under.

When Jewel comes up he has the saw.

When we pass the wagon pa is standing beside it, scrubbing at the two mud smears with a handful of leaves. Against the jungle Jewel's horse looks like a patchwork quilt hung on a line.

Cash has not moved. We stand above him, holding the plane, the saw, the hammer, the square, the rule, the chalk-line, while Dewey Dell squats and lifts Cash's head. 'Cash,' she says; 'Cash.'

He opens his eyes, staring profoundly up at our inverted faces.

'If ever was such a misfortunate man,' pa says.

'Look Cash,' we say, holding the tools up so he can see; 'what else did you have?'

He tries to speak, rolling his head, shutting his eyes.

'Cash,' we say; 'Cash.'

It is to vomit he is turning his head. Dewey Dell wipes

his mouth on the wet hem of her dress; then he can speak.

'It's his saw-set,' Jewel says. 'The new one he bought when he bought the rule.' He moves, turning away. Vernon looks up after him, still squatting. Then he rises and follows Jewel down to the water.

'If ever was such a misfortunate man,' pa says. He looms tall above us as we squat; he looks like a figure carved clumsily from tough wood by a drunken caricaturist. 'It's a trial,' he says. 'But I don't begrudge her it. No man can say I begrudge her it.' Dewey Dell has laid Cash's head back on the folded coat, twisting his head a little to avoid the vomit. Beside him his tools lie. 'A fellow might call it lucky it was the same leg he broke when he fell offen that church,' pa says. 'But I don't begrudge her it.'

Jewel and Vernon are in the river again. From here they do not appear to violate the surface at all, it is as though it had severed them both at a single blow, the two torsos moving with infinitesimal and ludicrous care upon the surface. It looks peaceful, like machinery does after you have watched it and listened to it for a long time. As though the clotting which is you had dissolved into the myriad original motion, and seeing and hearing in themselves blind and deaf; fury in itself quiet with stagnation. Squatting, Dewey Dell's wet dress shapes for the dead eyes of three blind men those mammalian ludicrosities which are the horizons and the valleys of the earth.

Cash

It wasn't on a balance. I told them that if they wanted it to tote and ride on a balance, they would have to—

Absalom, Absalom (1936)

Faulkner's finest complex plot is an absolutely full story
of the founding, establishment, decline and fall of the
dynastic design of Thomas Sutpen. It is a large-scale fable
of ambition thwarted by miscegenation, a map of inter-
sections between slavery, aristocratism, Civil War and
sexual purism in the South and the world. Quentin Compson tells his Canadian fellow student at Harvard, during
the bitter cold northern winter, all he can say of Sutpen's
design, out of information passed on from his family and
from a single incident in his own life. Within this line
Faulkner plays a web of reflexive space and time games
in order to reveal his subject fully. The first passage is
Quentin's memory of his father's information on Sutpen,
the involved sentences carrying the desire to penetrate to
interior meaning at every point, with Quentin and Shreve
interrupting to make sure they miss nothing. In the second
passage, Shreve has been rehearsing the story as Quentin
has told it to him. Now, both young men imagine themselves back in time to the point where Sutpen, a colonel
in the Confederate army, is visited by his son Henry—a
fine example of Faulkner's ability to create atmosphere

rapidly. In the centre of the Civil War, generations confront each other over the crux of racism: Judith is Henry's sister, and Charles Bon is his half-brother, who inherits 'Negro blood' from his mother. Clytie is Clytemnestra Sutpen, Thomas's daughter by a slave.

I

'Yes, the two children, the son and the daughter by sex and age so glib to the design that he might have planned that too, by character mental and physical so glib to it that he might have culled them out of the celestial herd of seraphs and cherubim like he chose his twenty niggers out of whatever swapping there must have been when he repudiated that first wife and that child when he discovered that they would not be adjunctive to the forwarding of that design. And Grandfather said there was no conscience about that, that Sutpen sat in the office that afternoon after thirty years and told him how his conscience had bothered him somewhat at first but that he had argued calmly and logically with his conscience until it was settled, just as he must have argued with his conscience about his and Mr Coldfield's bill of lading (only probably not as long here, since time here would be pressing) until that was settled— how he granted that by certain lights there was injustice in what he did but that he had obviated that as much as lay in his power by being aboveboard in the matter; that he could have simply deserted her, could have taken his hat and walked out, but he did not: and that he had what Grandfather would have to admit was a good and valid claim, if not to the whole place which he alone had saved, as well as the lives of all the white people on it, at least to that portion of it which had been specifically described and deeded to him in the marriage settlement which he had entered in good faith, with no reservations as to his obscure origin and material equipment, while there had been not only reservation but actual misrepresentation on their part and misrepresentation of such a crass nature as

to have not only voided and frustrated without his knowing it the central motivation of his entire design, but to
have made an ironic delusion of all that he had suffered
and endured in the past and all that he could ever accomplish in the future towards that design—which claim he
had voluntarily relinquished, taking only the twenty niggers out of all he might have claimed and which many
another man in his place would have insisted upon keeping
and (in which contention) would have been supported by
both legal and moral sanction even if not the delicate one
of conscience: and Grandfather not saying "Wait wait"
now because it was that innocence again, that innocence
which believed that the ingredients of morality were like
the ingredients of pie or cake and once you had measured
them and balanced them and mixed them and put them
into the oven it was all finished and nothing but pie or
cake could come out—Yes, sitting there in Grandfather's
office trying to explain with that patient amazed recapitula-
tion, not to Grandfather and not to himself because Grandfather said that his very calmness was indication that he
had long since given up any hope of ever understanding it,
but trying to explain to circumstance, to fate itself, the
logical steps by which he had arrived at a result absolutely
and forever incredible, repeating the clear and simple
synopsis of his history (which he and Grandfather both
now knew) as if he were trying to explain it to an in-
tractible and unpredictable child:
  ' "You see, I had a design in my mind. Whether it was a
good or bad design is beside the point the question is,
Where did I make the mistake in it, what did I do or misdo
in it, whom or what injure by it to the extent which this
would indicate. I had a design. To accomplish it I should
require money, a house, a plantation, slaves, a family—
incidentally of course, a wife. I set out to acquire these,
asking no favour of any man. I even risked my life at one
time, as I told you, though as I also told you I did not
undertake this risk purely and simply to gain a wife, though
it did have that result. But that is beside the point also:
suffice that I had a wife, accepted her in good faith, with

no reservations about myself, and I expected as much from them. I did not even demand, mind, as one of my obscure origin might have been expected to do (or at least be condoned in the doing) out of ignorance of gentility in dealing with gentleborn people. I did not demand; I accepted them at their own valuation while insisting on my own part upon explaining fully about myself and my progenitors: yet they deliberately withheld from me the one fact which I have reason to know they were aware would have caused me to decline the entire matter, otherwise they would not have withheld it from me—a fact which I did not learn until after my son was born. And even then I did not act hastily. I could have reminded them of these wasted years, these years which would now leave me behind with my schedule not only the amount of elapsed time which their number represented, but that compensatory amount of time represented by their number which I should now have to spend to advance myself once more to the point I had reached and lost. But I did not. I merely explained how this new fact rendered it impossible that this woman and child be incorporated in my design, and following which, as I told you, I made no attempt to keep not only that which I might consider myself to have earned at the risk of my life but which had been given to me by signed testimonials, but on the contrary I declined and resigned all right and claim to this in order that I might repair whatever injustice I might be considered to have done by so providing for the two persons whom I might be considered to have deprived of anything I might later possess: and this was agreed to, mind; agreed to between the two parties. And yet, and after more than thirty years, more than thirty years after my conscience had finally assured me that if I had done an injustice, I had done what I could to rectify it—" and Grandfather not saying "Wait" now but saying, hollering maybe even: "Conscience? Conscience? Good God, man, what else did you expect? Didn't the very affinity and instinct for misfortune of a man who had spent that much time in a monastery even, let alone one who had lived that many years as you lived them, tell you better than that? didn't the dread and fear of females which you must have drawn in with the primary mammalian milk teach you better? What kind of abysmal and purblind innocence could that have been which someone told you to call virginity? what conscience to trade with which would have warranted you in the belief that you could have bought immunity from her for no other coin but justice?"—'

It was at this point that Shreve went to the bedroom and put on the bathrobe. He did not say Wait, he just rose and left Quentin sitting before the table, the open book and the letter, and went out and returned in the robe and sat again and took up the cold pipe, though without filling it anew or lighting it as it was. 'All right,' he said. 'So that Christmas Henry brought him home, into the house, and the demon looked up and saw the face he believed he had paid off and discharged twenty-eight years ago. Go on.'

'Yes,' Quentin said. 'Father said he probably named him himself. Charles Bon. Charles Good. He didn't tell Grandfather that he did, but Grandfather believed he did, would have. That would have been a part of the cleaning up, just as he would have done his share towards cleaning up the exploded caps and musket cartridges after the siege if he hadn't been sick (or maybe engaged); he would have insisted on it maybe, the conscience again which could not allow her and the child any place in the design even though he could have closed his eyes and, if not fooled the rest of the world as they had fooled him, at least have frightened any man out of speaking the secret aloud—the same conscience which would not permit the child, since it was a boy, to bear either his name or that of its maternal grandfather, yet which would also forbid him to do the customary and provide a quick husband for the discarded woman and so give his son an authentic name. He chose the name himself, Grandfather believed, just as he named them all —the Charles Goods and the Clytemnestras and Henry and Judith and all of them—that entire fecundity of dragons' teeth as father called it. And Father said—'

'Your father,' Shreve said. 'He seems to have got an

awful lot of delayed information awful quick, after having
waited forty-five years. If he knew all this, what was his
reason for telling you that the trouble between Henry and
Bon was the octoroon woman?'

'He didn't know it then. Grandfather didn't tell him all
of it either, like Sutpen never told Grandfather quite all of
it.'

'Then who did tell him?'

'I did.' Quentin did not move, did not look up while
Shreve watched him. 'The day after we—after that night
when we—'

'Oh,' Shreve said. 'After you and the old aunt. I see. Go
on. And father said—'

'—said how he must have stood there on the front gallery that afternoon and waited for Henry and the friend
Henry had been writing home about all fail to come up the
drive, and that maybe after Henry wrote the name in the
first letter Sutpen probably told himself it couldn't be, that
there was a limit even to irony beyond which it became
either just vicious but not fatal horseplay or harmless coincidence, since Father said that even Sutpen probably
knew that nobody yet ever invented a name that somebody
didn't own now or hadn't owned once: and they rode up
at last and Henry said, "Father, this is Charles" and he—'
('the demon,' Shreve said) '—saw the face and knew that
there are situations where coincidence is no more than the
little child that rushes out onto a football field to take part
in the game and the players run over and around the un-
scathed head and go on and shock together, and in the fury
of the struggle for the facts called gain or loss nobody even
remembers the child nor saw who came and snatched it
back from dissolution—that he stood there at his own
door, just as he had imagined, planned, designed, and sure
enough and after fifty years the forlorn nameless and home-
less lost child came to knock at it and no monkey-dressed
nigger anywhere under the sun to come to the door and
order the child away; and Father said that even then, even
though he knew that Bon and Judith had never laid eyes
on one another, he must have felt and heard the design—

house, position, posterity and all—come down like it had been built out of smoke, making no sound, creating no rush of displaced air and not even leaving any debris. And he not calling it retribution, no sins of the father come home to roost; not even calling it bad luck but just a mistake: that mistake which he could not discover himself and which he came to Grandfather, not to excuse but just to review the facts for an impartial (and Grandfather said he believed, a legally trained) mind to examine and find and point out to him. Not moral retribution you see: just an old mistake in fact which a man of courage and shrewdness (the one of which he now knew he possessed, the other of which he believed that he had now learned, acquired) could still combat if he could only find out what the mistake had been. Because he did not give up. He never did give up; Grandfather said that his subsequent actions (the fact that for a time he did nothing and so perhaps helped to bring about the very situation which he dreaded) were not the result of any failing of courage or shrewdness or ruthlessness, but were the result of his conviction that it had all come from a mistake and until he discovered what that mistake had been he did not intend to risk making another one.'

II

Shreve ceased again. It was just as well, since he had no listener. Perhaps he was aware of it. Then suddenly he had no talker either, though possibly he was not aware of this. Because now neither of them were there. They were both in Carolina and the time was forty-six years ago, and it was not even four now but compounded still further, since now both of them were Henry Sutpen and both of them were Bon, compounded each of both yet either neither, smelling the very smoke which had blown and faded away forty-six years ago from the *bivouac fires burning in a pine grove, the gaunt and ragged men sitting or lying about them, talking not about the war yet all curiously enough (or perhaps*

*not curiously at all) facing the South where further on in
the darkness the pickets stood—the pickets who, watching
to the South, could see the flicker and gleam of the Federal
bivouac fires myriad and faint and encircling half the
horizon and counting ten fires for each Confederate one,
and between whom and which (Rebel picket and Yankee
fire) the Yankee outposts watched the darkness also, the
two picket lines so close that each could hear the challenge
of the other's officers passing from post to post and dying
away: and when gone, the voice, invisible, cautious, not
loud yet carrying:*

—Hey, Reb.

—Yah.

—Where you fellers going?

—Richmond.

—So are we. Why not wait for us?

—We air.

*The men about the fires would not hear this exchange,
though they would presently hear the orderly plainly
enough as he passes from fire to fire, asking for Sutpen and
being directed on and so reaches the fire at last, the smoldering log, with his monotonous speech: 'Sutpen? I'm looking
for Sutpen' until Henry sits up and says, 'Here.' He is
gaunt and ragged and unshaven; because of the last four
years and because he had not quite got his height when
the four years began, he is not as tall by two inches as he
gave promise of being, and not as heavy by thirty pounds
as he probably will be a few years after he has outlived
the four years, if he do outlive them.*

—Here, he says—What is it?

—The colonel wants you.

*The orderly does not return with him. Instead, he walks
alone through the darkness along a rutted road, a road
rutted and cut and churned where the guns have passed
over it that afternoon, and reaches the tent at last, one of
the few tents, the canvas wall gleaming faintly from a
candle within, the silhouette of a sentry before it, who
challenges him.*

—Sutpen, Henry says—The colonel sent for me.

*The sentry gestures him into the tent. He stoops through
the entrance, the canvas falls behind him as someone, the
only occupant of the tent, rises from a camp chair behind
the table on which the candle sits, his shadow swooping
high and huge up the canvas wall. He (Henry) comes to
salute facing a gray sleeve with a colonel's braid on it, one
bearded cheek, a jutting nose, a shaggy droop of iron-
riddle hair—a face which Henry does not recognize, not
because he has not seen it in four years and does not expect to see it here and now, but rather because he is not
looking at it. He just salutes the braided cuff and stands so
until the other says,*

—Henry.

*Even now Henry does not start. He just stands so, the
two of them stand so, looking at one another. It is the older
man who moves first, though they meet in the center of
the tent, where they embrace and kiss before Henry is
aware that he has moved, was going to move, moved by
what of close blood which in the reflex instant abrogates
and reconciles even though it does not yet (perhaps never
will) forgive, who stands now while his father holds his
face between both hands, looking at it.*

—Henry, *Sutpen says*—My son.

*Then they sit, one on either side of the table, in the
chairs reserved for officers, the table (an open map lies on
it) and the candle between them.*

—You were at Shiloh, Colonel Willows tells me, *Sutpen says.*

—Yes, sir, *Henry says.*

*He is about to say Charles carried me back but he does
not, because already he knows what is coming. He does not
even think Surely Judith didn't write him about that letter
or It was Clytie who sent him word somehow that Charles
has written her. He thinks neither of these. To him it is
logical and natural that their father should know of his
and Bon's decision: that rapport of blood which should
bring Bon to decide to write, himself to agree to it and
their father to know of it at the same identical instant,
after a period of four years, out of all time. Now it does*

come, almost exactly as he had known that it will:

—I have seen Charles Bon, Henry.

Henry says nothing. It is coming now. He says nothing, he merely stares at his father—the two of them in leaf-faded gray, a single candle, a crude tent walling them away from a darkness where alert pickets face one another and where weary men sleep without shelter, waiting for dawn and the firing, the weary backward walking to commence again: yet in a second tent candle gray and all are gone and it is the holly-decked Christmas library at Sutpen's Hundred four years ago and the table not a camp table suitable for the spreading of maps but the heavy carved rosewood one at home with the group photograph of his mother and sister and himself sitting upon it, his father behind the table and behind his father the window above the garden where Judith and Bon strolled in that slow rhythm where the heat matches the footsteps and the eyes need only look at one another.

—You are going to let him marry Judith, Henry.

Still Henry does not answer. It has all been said before, and now he has had four years of bitter struggle following which, whether it be victory or defeat which he has gained, at least he has gained it and has peace now, even if the peace be mostly despair.

—He cannot marry her, Henry.

Now Henry speaks.

—You said that before. I told you then. And now, and now it wont be much longer now and then we wont have anything left: honor nor pride nor God since God quit us four years ago only He never thought it necessary to tell us; no shoes nor clothes and no need for them; not only no land to make food out of but no need for the food and when you dont have God and honor and pride, nothing matters except that there is the old mindless meat that dont even care if it was defeat or victory, that wont even die, that will be out in the woods and fields, grubbing up roots and weeds—Yes. I have decided. Brother or not, I have decided. I will. I will.

—He must not marry her, Henry.

57

—Yes. I said at first, but I was not decided then. I didn't let him. But now I have had four years to decide in. I will. I am going to.

—He must not marry her, Henry. His mother's father told me that her mother had been a Spanish woman. I believed him; it was not until after he was born that I found out that his mother was part negro.

Nor did Henry ever say that he did not remember leaving the tent. He remembers all of it. He remembers stooping through the entrance again and passing the sentry again; he remembers walking back down the cut and rutted road, stumbling in the dark among the ruts on either side of which the fires have now died to embers, so that he can barely distinguish the men sleeping on the earth about them. *It must be better than eleven o'clock,* he thinks. *And another eight miles tomorrow. If it were only not for those damned guns. Why doesn't Old Joe give the guns to Sherman. Then we could make twenty miles a day. We could join Lee then. At least Lee stops and fights some of the time.* He remembers it. He remembers how he did not return to his fire but stopped presently in a lonely place and leaned against a pine, leaning quietly and easily, with his head back so he could look up at the shabby shaggy branches like something in wrought iron spreading motionless against the chill vivid stars of early spring, thinking *I hope he remembers to thank Colonel Willow for letting us use his tent.* thinking not what he would do but what he would have to do. Because he knew what he would do; it now depended on what Bon would do, would force him to do, since he knew that he would do it. *So I must go to him,* he thought, thinking, *Now it is better than two oclock and it will be dawn soon.*

Then it was dawn, or almost, and it was cold: a chill which struck through the worn patched thin clothing, through the something of weariness and undernourishment; the passive ability, not the volitional will, to endure; there was light somewhere, enough of it for him to distinguish Bon's sleeping face from among the others where he lay wrapped in his blankets, beneath his spread cloak; enough light for him to wake Bon by and for Bon to distinguish his face (or perhaps something communicated by Henry's hand) because Bon does not speak, demand to know who it is: he merely rises and puts the cloak about his shoulders and approaches the smoldering fire and is kicking it into a blaze when Henry speaks:

—Wait.

Bon pauses and looks at Henry; now he can see Henry's face. He says,

—You will be cold. You are cold now. You haven't been asleep, have you? Here.

He swings the cloak from his shoulders and holds it out.

—No, Henry says.

—Yes. Take it. I'll get my blanket.

Bon puts the cloak about Henry and goes and takes up his tumbled blanket and swings it about his shoulders, and they move aside and sit on a log. Now it is dawn. The east is gray; it will be primrose soon and then red with firing and once more the weary backward marching will begin, retreating from annihilation, falling back upon defeat, though not quite yet. There will be a little time yet for them to sit side by side upon the log in the making light of dawn, the one in the cloak, the other in the blanket; their voices are not much louder than the silent dawn itself:

—So it's the miscegenation, not the incest, which you cant bear.

Henry doesn't answer.

—And he sent me no word? He did not ask you to send me to him? No word to me, no word at all? That was all he had to do, now, today; four years ago or at any time during the four years. That was all. He would not have needed to ask it, require it, of me. I would have offered it. I would have said, I will never see her again before he could have asked it of me. He did not have to do this, Henry. He didn't need to tell you I am a nigger to stop me. He could have stopped me without that, Henry.

—No! Henry cries.—No! No! I will—I'll—

He springs up; his face is working; Bon can see his teeth within the soft beard which covers his sunken cheeks, and the whites of Henry's eyes as though the eyeballs struggled in their sockets as the panting breath struggled in his lungs —the panting which ceased, the breath held, the eyes too looking down at him where he sat on the log, the voice now not much louder than an expelled breath:

—You said, could have stopped you. What do you mean by that?

Now it is Bon who does not answer, who sits on the log looking at the face stooped above him. Henry says, still in that voice no louder than breathing:

—But now? You mean you—

—Yes. What else can I do now? I gave him the choice. I have been giving him the choice for four years.

—Think of her. Not of me: of her.

—I have. For four years. Of you and her. Now I am thinking of myself.

—No, Henry says.—No. No.

—I cannot?

—You shall not.

—Who will stop me, Henry?

—No, Henry says.—No. No. No.

Now it is Bon who watches Henry; he can see the whites of Henry's eyes again as he sits looking at Henry with that expression which might be called smiling. His hand vanishes beneath the blanket and reappears, holding his pistol by the barrel, the butt extended toward Henry.

—Then do it now, he says.

Henry looks at the pistol; now he is not only panting, he is trembling; when he speaks now his voice is not even the exhalation, it is the suffused and suffocating inbreath itself:

—You are my brother.

—No I'm not. I'm the nigger that's going to sleep with your sister. Unless you stop me Henry.

Suddenly Henry grasps the pistol, jerks it free of Bon's hand stands so, the pistol in his hand, panting and panting; again Bon can see the whites of his inrolled eyes while he sits on the log and watches Henry with that faint expres-

sion about the eyes and mouth which might be smiling.

—Do it now, Henry, he says.

Henry whirls; in the same motion he hurls the pistol from him and stops again, gripping Bon by both shoulders, panting.

—You shall not! he says—You shall not! Do you hear me?

Bon does not move beneath the gripping hands; he sits motionless, with his faint fixed grimace; his voice is gentler than that first breath in which the pine branches begin to move a little:

—You will have to stop me, Henry. 'And he never slipped away,' Shreve said. 'He could have, but he never even tried. Jesus, maybe he even went to Henry and said, "I'm going Henry" and maybe they left together and rode side by side dodging Yankee patrols all the way back to Mississippi and right up to that gate; side by side and it only then that one of them ever rode ahead or dropped behind and that only then Henry spurred ahead and turned his horse to face Bon and took the pistol; and Judith and Clytie heard the shot, and maybe Wash Jones was hanging around somewhere in the back yard and so he was there to help Clytie and Judith carry him into the house and lay him on the bed, and Wash went to the town to tell the Aunt Rosa and the Aunt Rosa comes boiling out that afternoon and finds Judith standing without a tear before the closed door, holding the metal case she had given him with her picture in it but that didn't have her picture in it now but that of the octoroon and the kid. And your old man wouldn't know about that too: why the black son of a bitch should have taken her picture out and put the octoroon's picture in, so he invented a reason for it. But I know. And you know too. Dont you? Dont you, huh?' He glared at Quentin, leaning forward over the table now, looking huge and shapeless as a bear in his swaddling of garments. 'Don't you know? It was because he said to himself "If Henry dont mean what he said, it will be all right; I can take it out and destroy it. But if he does mean what he said, it will be the only way I will

61

have to say to her, *I was no good; do not grieve for me."* Aint that right; Aint it? By God, aint it?'

'Yes,' Quentin said.

'Come on,' Shreve said. 'Let's get out of this refrigerator and go to bed.'

Go Down, Moses (1942)

The first episode describes the inheritance of Ike McCaslin from the hunter whose knowledge of the wilderness is to be Ike's initiation into the meaning of the land. Fathers is part Chickasaw, part white, part black: it is his skill and dignified integrity that gives him his status in Yoknapatawpha. The second passage describes that part of the hunt for the bear, Old Ben, in which Ike is most involved as he stands on the threshold of manhood. In the last passage, Faulkner's huge sentences encompass Ike's later monologue, as a young man, in the presence of his cousin and guardian who has just spoken of 'truth so mazed for them that spoke it and so confused for them that heard it yet still there was 1865'. That is, after all the complexity of struggle to make the South, there was still the Civil War to defeat them. It is here, in 'The Bear', that Faulkner comes nearest to Ike's sense of his Southern inheritance—that backlog of slavery, land and money grabbing, and coarse sexuality which he will finally renounce.

The Old People

I

At first there was nothing. There was the faint, cold, steady rain, the grey and constant light of the late November dawn, with the voices of the hounds converging somewhere in it and towards them. Then Sam Fathers, standing just behind the boy as he had been standing when the boy shot his first running rabbit with his first gun and almost with the first load it ever carried, touched his shoulder and he began to shake, not with any cold. Then the buck was there. He did not come into sight; he was just there, looking not like a ghost but as if all of light were condensed in him and he were the source of it, not only moving in it but disseminating it, already running, seen first as you always see the deer, in that split second after he has already seen you, already slanting away in that first soaring bound, the antlers even in that dim light looking like a small rocking-chair balanced on his head.

'Now,' Sam Fathers said, 'shoot quick, and slow.'

The boy did not remember that shot at all. He would live to be eighty, as his father and his father's twin brother and their father in his turn had lived to be, but he would never hear that shot nor remember even the shock of the gun-butt. He didn't even remember what he did with the gun afterwards. He was running. Then he was standing over the buck where it lay on the wet earth still in the attitude of speed and not looking at all dead, standing over it shaking and jerking, with Sam Fathers beside him again, extending the knife. 'Dont walk up to him in front,' Sam said. 'If he aint dead, he will cut you all to pieces with his feet. Walk up to him from behind and take him by the horn first, so you can hold his head down until you can jump away. Then slip your other hand down and hook your fingers in his nostrils.'

The boy did that—drew the head back and the throat taut and drew Sam Fathers knife across the throat and Sam stooped and dipped his hands in the hot smoking blood and wiped them back and forth across the boy's face. Then Sam's horn rang in the wet grey woods and again and again; there was a boiling wave of dogs about them, with Tennie's Jim and Boon Hogganbeck whipping them back after each had had a taste of the blood, then the men, the true hunters—Walter Ewell whose rifle never missed, and Major de Spain and old General Compson and the boy's cousin, McCaslin Edmonds, grandson of his father's sister, sixteen years his senior and, since both he and McCaslin were only children and the boy's father had been nearing seventy when he was born, more his brother than his cousin and more his father than either—sitting their horses and looking down at them: at the old man of seventy who had been a negro for two generations now but whose face and bearing were still those of the Chickasaw chief who had been his father; and the white boy of twelve with the prints of the bloody hands on his face, who had nothing to do now but stand straight and not let the trembling show.

'Did he do it all right, Sam?' his cousin McCaslin said.

'He done all right,' Sam Fathers said.

They were the white boy, marked for ever, and the old dark man sired on both sides by savage kings, who had marked him, whose bloody hands had merely formally consecrated him to that which, under the man's tutelage, he had already accepted, humbly and joyfully, with abnegation and with pride too; the hands, the touch, the first worthy blood which he had been found at last worthy to draw, joining him and the man for ever, so that the man would continue to live past the boy's seventy years and then eighty years, long after the man himself had entered the earth as chiefs and kings entered it—the child, not yet a man, whose grandfather had lived in the same country and in almost the same manner as the boy himself would grow up to live, leaving his descendants in the land in his turn as his grandfather had done, and the old man past seventy whose grandfathers had owned the land long before the white man ever saw it and who had vanished from it now with all their kind, what of blood they left behind them running now in another race and for a while even in bondage and now drawing towards the end of its alien and irrevocable course, barren, since Sam Fathers had no children.

His father was Ikkemotubbe himself, who had named himself Doom. Sam told the boy about that—how Ikkemotubbe, old Issetibbeha's sister's son, had run away to New Orleans in his youth and returned seven years later with a French companion calling himself the Chevalier Soeur-Blonde de Vitry, who must have been the Ikkemotubbe of his family too and who was already addressing Ikkemotubbe as *Du Homme*—returned, came home again, with his foreign Aramis and the quadroon slave woman who was to be Sam's mother, and a gold-laced hat and coat and a wicker wine-hamper containing a litter of month-old puppies and a gold snuff-box filled with a white powder resembling fine sugar. And how he was met at the River landing by three or four companions of his bachelor youth, and while the light of a smoking torch gleamed on the glittering braid of the hat and coat Doom squatted in the mud of the land and took one of the puppies from the hamper and put a pinch of the white powder on its tongue and the puppy died before the one who was holding it could cast it away. And how they returned to the Plantation where Issetibbeha, dead now, had been succeeded by his son, Doom's fat cousin Moketubbe, and the next day Moketubbe's eight-year-old son died suddenly and that afternoon, in the presence of Moketubbe and most of the others (the People, Sam Fathers called them) Doom produced another puppy from the wine-hamper and put a pinch of the white powder on its tongue and Moketubbe abdicated and Doom became in fact The Man which his French friend already called him. And how on the day after that, during the ceremony of accession, Doom pronounced a marriage between the pregnant quadroon and one of the slave men which he had just inherited (that was how Sam Fathers got his name, which in Chickasaw had been Had-Two-Fathers) and two years later sold the man and woman and the child who was his own son to his white neighbour, Carothers McCaslin.

That was seventy years ago. The Sam Fathers whom the boy knew was already sixty—a man not tall, squat rather, almost sedentary, flabby-looking though he actually was not, with hair like a horse's main which even at seventy showed no trace of white and a face which showed no age until he smiled, whose only visible trace of negro blood was a slight dullness of the hair and the fingernails, and something else which you did notice about the eyes, which you noticed because it was not always there, only in repose and not always then—something not in their shape nor pigment but in their expression, and the boy's cousin McCaslin told him what that was: not the heritage of Ham, not the mark of servitude but of bondage; the knowledge that for a while that part of his blood had been the blood of slaves. 'Like an old lion or a bear in a cage,' McCaslin said. 'He was born in the cage and has been in it all his life; he knows nothing else. Then he smells something. It might be anything, any breeze blowing past anything and then into his nostrils. But there for a second was the hot sand or the cane-brake that he never even saw himself, might not even know if he did see it and probably does know he couldn't hold his own with it if he got back to it. But that's not what he smells then. It was the cage he smelled. He hadn't smelled the cage until that minute. Then the hot sand or the brake blew into his nostrils and blew away, and all he could smell was the cage. That's what makes his eyes look like that.'

'Then let him go!' the boy cried. 'Let him go!'

His cousin laughed shortly. Then he stopped laughing, making the sound that is. It had never been laughing. 'His cage aint McCaslins,' he said. 'He was a wild man. When he was born, all his blood on both sides, except the little white part, knew things that had been tamed out of our blood so long ago that we have not only forgotten them, we have to live together in herds to protect ourselves from our own sources. He was the direct son not only of a warrior but of a chief. Then he grew up and began to learn things, and all of a sudden one day he found out that he

67

had been betrayed, the blood of the warriors and chiefs had been betrayed. Not by his father,' he added quickly. 'He probably never held it against old Doom for selling him and his mother into slavery, because he probably believed the damage was already done before then and it was the same warriors' and chiefs' blood in him and Doom both that was betrayed through the black blood and not wilfully betrayed by his mother, but betrayed by her all the same, who had bequeathed him not only the blood of slaves but even a little of the very blood which had enslaved it; himself his own battleground, the scene of his own vanquishment and the mausoleum of his defeat. His cage aint us,' McCaslin said. 'Did you ever know anybody yet, even your father and Uncle Buddy, that ever told him to do or not to do anything that he ever paid any attention to?'

That was true. The boy first remembered him as sitting in the door of the plantation blacksmith's shop, where he sharpened plough-points and mended tools and even did rough carpenter-work when he was not in the woods. And sometimes, even when the woods had not drawn him, even with the shop cluttered with work which the farm waited on, Sam would sit there, doing nothing at all for half a day or a whole one, and no man, neither the boy's father and twin uncle in their day nor his cousin McCaslin after he became practical though not yet titular master, ever to say to him, 'I want this finished by sundown' or 'why wasn't this done yesterday?' And once each year, in the late fall, in November, the boy would watch the wagon, the hooped canvas top erected now, being loaded—the food, hams, and sausages from the smokehouse, coffee and flour and molasses from the commissary, a whole beef killed just last night for the dogs until there would be meat in camp, the crate containing the dogs themselves, then the bedding, the guns, the horns and lanterns and axes, and his cousin McCaslin and Sam Fathers in their hunting clothes would mount to the seat and with Tennie's Jim sitting on the dog-crate they would drive away to Jefferson, to join Major de Spain and General Compson and

Boon Hogganbeck and Walter Ewell and go on into the big bottom of the Tallahatchie where the deer and bear were, to be gone two weeks. But before the wagon was even loaded the boy would find that he could watch no longer. He would go away, running almost, to stand behind the corner where he could not see the wagon and nobody could see him, not crying, holding himself rigid except for the trembling, whispering to himself: 'Soon now. Soon now. Just three more years' (or two more or one more) 'and I will be ten. Then Cass said I can go.'

White man's work, when Sam did work. Because he did nothing else: farmed no allotted acres of his own, as the other ex-slaves of old Carothers McCaslin did, performed no fieldwork for daily wages as the younger and newer negroes did—and the boy never knew just how that had been settled between Sam and old Carothers, or perhaps with old Carothers's twin sons after him. For, although Sam lived among the negroes, in a cabin among the other cabins in the quarters, and consorted with negroes (what of consorting with anyone Sam did after the boy got big enough to walk alone from the house to the blacksmith's shop and then to carry a gun) and dressed like them and talked like them and even went with them to the negro church now and then, he was still the son of that Chickasaw chief and the negroes knew it. And, it seemed to the boy, not only negroes. Boon Hogganbeck's grandmother had been a Chickasaw woman too, and although the blood had run white since and Boon was a white man, it was not chief's blood. To the boy at least, the difference was apparent immediately you saw Boon and Sam together, and even Boon seemed to know it was there—even Boon, to whom in his tradition it had never occurred that anyone might be better born than himself. A man might be smarter, he admitted that, or richer (luckier, he called it) but not better born. Boon was a mastiff, absolutely faithful, dividing his fidelity equally between Major de Spain and the boy's cousin McCaslin, absolutely dependent for his very bread and dividing that impartially too between Major de Spain and McCaslin, hardy, generous, courageous enough, a slave

to all the appetites and almost unratiocinative. In the boy's
eyes at least it was Sam Fathers, the negro, who bore himself not only towards his cousin McCaslin and Major de
Spain but towards all white men, with gravity and dignity
and without servility or recourse to that impenetrable wall
of ready and easy mirth which negroes sustain between
themselves and white men, bearing himself towards his
cousin McCaslin not only as one man to another but as an
older man to a younger.

He taught the boy the woods, to hunt, when to shoot and
when not to shoot, when to kill and when not to kill, and
better, what to do with it afterward. Then he would talk
to the boy, the two of them sitting beneath the close fierce
stars on a summer hilltop while they waited for the hounds
to bring the fox back within hearing, or beside a fire
in the November or December woods while the dogs
worked out a coon's trail along the creek, or fireless in the
pitch black and heavy dew of April mornings while they
squatted beneath a turkey-roost. The boy would never
question him; Sam did not react to questions. The boy
would just wait and then listen and Sam would begin,
talking about the old days and the People whom he had not
had time ever to know and so could not remember (he did
not remember ever having seen his father's face), and in
place of whom the other race into which his blood had run
supplied him with no substitute.

And as he talked about those old times and those dead
and vanished men of another race from either that the boy
knew, gradually to the boy those times would cease to
be old times and would become a part of the boy's present,
not only as if they had happened yesterday but as if they
were still happening, the men who walked through them
actually walking in breath and air and casting an actual
shadow on the earth they had not quitted. And more: as
if some of them had not happened yet but would occur tomorrow, until at last it would seem to the boy that he himself had not come into existence yet, that none of his race
nor the other subject race which his people had brought
with them into the land had come here yet; that although

it had been his grandfather's and then his father's and uncle's and was now his cousin's and someday would be his own land which he and Sam hunted over, their hold upon it actually was as trivial and without reality as the now faded and archaic script in the chancery book in Jefferson which allocated it to them and that it was he, the boy, who was the guest here and Sam Father's voice the mouthpiece of the host.

Until three years ago there had been two of them, the other a full-blood Chickasaw, in a sense even more incredibly lost than Sam Fathers. He called himself Jobaker, as if it were one word. Nobody knew his history at all. He was a hermit, living in a foul little shack at the forks of the creek five miles from the plantation and about that far from any other habitation. He was a market hunter and fisherman and he consorted with nobody, black or white; no negro would even cross his path and no man dared approach his hut except Sam. And perhaps once a month the boy would find them in Sam's shop—two old men squatting on their heels on the dirt floor, talking in a mixture of negroid English and flat hill dialect and now and then a phrase of that old tongue which as time went on and the boy squatted there too listening, he began to learn. Then Jobaker died. That is, nobody had seen him for some time. Then one morning Sam was missing, nobody, not even the boy, knew when nor where, until that night when some negroes hunting in the creek bottom saw the sudden burst of flame and approached. It was Jobaker's hut, but before they got anywhere near it, someone shot at them from the shadows beyond it. It was Sam who fired, but nobody ever found Jobaker's grave.

The next morning, sitting at breakfast with his cousin, the boy saw Sam pass the dining-room window and he remembered then that never in his life before had he seen Sam nearer the house than the blacksmith's shop. He stopped eating even; he sat there and he and his cousin both heard voices from beyond the pantry door, then the door opened and Sam entered, carrying his hat in his hand but without knocking as anyone else on the place except a house servant would have done, entered just far enough for the door to close behind him and stood looking at neither of them—the Indian face above the nigger clothes, looking at something over their heads or at something not even in the room.

'I want to go,' he said. 'I want to go to the Big Bottom to live.'

'To live?' the boy's cousin said.

'At Major de Spain's and your camp, where you go to hunt,' Sam said. 'I could take care of it for you all while you aint there. I will build me a little house in the woods, if you rather I didn't stay in the big one.'

'What about Isaac here?' his cousin said. 'How will you get away from him? Are you going to take him with you?' But still Sam looked at neither of them, standing just inside the room with that face that showed nothing, which showed that he was an old man only when it smiled.

'I want to go,' he said. 'Let me go.'

'Yes,' the cousin said quietly. 'Of course. I'll fix it with Major de Spain. You want to go soon?'

'I'm going now,' Sam said. He went out. And that was all. The boy was nine then; it seemed perfectly natural that nobody, not even his cousin McCaslin, should argue with Sam. Also, since he was nine now, he could understand that Sam could leave him and their days and nights in the woods together without any wrench. He believed that he and Sam both knew that this was not only temporary but that the exigencies of his maturing, of that for which Sam had been training him all his life some day to dedicate himself, required it. They had settled that one night last summer while he listened to the hounds bringing a fox back up the creek valley; now the boy discerned in that very talk under the high, fierce August stars a presage, a warning, of this moment, today. 'I done taught you all there is of this settled country,' Sam said. 'You can hunt it good as I can now. You are ready for the Big Bottom now, for bear and deer. Hunter's meat,' he said. 'Next year you will be ten. You will write your age in two numbers and you will be ready to become a man. Your pa' (Sam always referred to the boy's cousin as his father, establishing even before the boy's orphanhood did that relationship between them not of the ward to his guardian and kinsman and chief and head of his blood, but of the child to the man who sired his flesh and his thinking too.) 'promised you can go with us then.' So the boy could understand Sam's going. But he couldn't understand why now, in March, six months before the moon for hunting...

The Bear

II

The next morning they started three hours earlier than they had ever done. Even Uncle Ash went, the cook, who called himself by profession a camp cook and who did little else save cook for Major de Spain's hunting and camping parties, yet who had been marked by the wilderness from simple juxtaposition to it until he responded as they all did, even the boy who until two weeks ago had never seen the wilderness, to a hound's ripped ear and shoulder and the print of a crooked foot in a patch of wet earth. They rode. It was too far to walk: the boy and Sam and Uncle Ash in the wagon with the dogs, his cousin and Major de Spain and General Compson and Boon and Walter and Tennie's Jim riding double on the horses; again the first grey light found him, as on that first morning two weeks ago, on the stand where Sam had placed and left him. With the gun which was too big for him, the breech-loader which did not even belong to him but to Major de Spain and which he had fired only once, at a stump on the first day to learn the recoil and how to reload it with the paper shells, he stood against a big gum tree beside a little bayou whose black still water crept without motion out of a cane-brake, across a small clearing and into the cane again, where, invisible, a bird, the big woodpecker called Lord-to-God by negroes, clattered at a dead trunk. It was a stand like any other stand, dissimilar only in incidentals to the one where he had stood each morning for two weeks; a territory new to him yet no less familiar than that other one which after two weeks he had come to believe he knew a little—the same solitude, the same loneliness through which frail and timorous man had merely passed without altering it, leaving no mark or scar, which looked exactly as it must have looked when the first ancestor of Sam Father's Chickasaw predecessors crept into it and looked about him, club or stone axe or bone arrow drawn and ready, different only because, squatting at the edge of the kitchen, he had smelled the dogs huddled and cringing beneath it and saw the raked ear and side of the bitch that, as Sam had said, had to be brave once in order to keep on calling herself a dog, and saw yesterday in the earth beside the gutted log, the print of the living foot. He heard no dogs at all. He never did certainly hear them. He only heard the drumming of the woodpecker stop short off, and knew that the bear was looking at him. He never saw it. He did not know whether it was facing him from the cane or behind him. He did not move, holding the useless gun which he knew now he would never fire at it, now or ever, tasting in his saliva that taint of brass which he had smelled in the huddled dogs when he peered under the kitchen.

Then it was gone. As abruptly as it had stopped, the woodpecker's dry hammering set up again, and after a while he believed he even heard the dogs—a murmur, scarce a sound even, which he had probably been hearing for a time, perhaps a minute or two, before he remarked it, drifting into hearing and then out again, dying away. They came nowhere near him. If it was dogs he heard, he could not have sworn to it; if it was a bear they ran, it was another bear. It was Sam himself who emerged from the cane and crossed the bayou, the injured bitch following at heel as a bird dog is taught to walk. She came and crouched against his leg, trembling. 'I didn't see him,' he said. 'I didn't, Sam.'

'I know it,' Sam said. 'He done the looking. You didn't hear him neither, did you?'

'No,' the boy said, 'I—'

'He's smart,' Sam said. 'Too smart.' Again the boy saw in his eyes that quality of dark and brooding lambence as Sam looked down at the bitch trembling faintly and steadily against the boy's leg. From her raked shoulder a few drops of fresh blood clung like bright berries. 'Too big. We ain't got the dog yet. But maybe some day.'

Because there would be a next time, after and after. He was only ten. It seemed to him that he could see them, the two of them, shadowy in the limbo form from which time emerged and became time: the old bear absolved of mortality and himself who shared a little of it. Because he recognized now what he had smelled in the huddled dogs and tasted in his own saliva, recognized fear as a boy, a youth, recognizes the existence of love and passion and experience which is his heritage but not yet his patrimony, from entering by chance the presence or perhaps even merely the bedroom of a woman who has loved and been loved by many men. *So I will have to see him,* he thought, without dread or even hope. *I will have to look at him.*

So it was in June of the next summer. They were at the camp again, celebrating Major de Spain's and General Compson's birthdays. Although the one had been born in September and the other in the depth of winter and almost thirty years earlier, each June the two of them and McCaslin and Boon and Walter Ewell (and the boy too from now on) spent two weeks at the camp, fishing and shooting squirrels and turkey and running coons and wildcats with the dogs at night. That is, Boon and the negroes (and the boy too now) fished and shot squirrels and ran the coons and cats, because the proven hunters, not only Major de Spain and old General Compson (who spent those two weeks sitting in a rocking-chair before a tremendous iron pot of Brunswick stew, stirring and tasting, with Uncle Ash to quarrel about how he was making it and Tennie's Jim to pour whisky into the tin dipper from which he drank it) but even McCaslin and Walter Ewell, who were still young enough, scorned such other than shooting the wild gobblers with pistols for wagers or to test their marksmanship.

That is, his cousin McCaslin and the others thought he

was hunting squirrels. Until the third evening he believed that Sam Fathers thought so too. Each morning he would leave the camp right after breakfast. He had his own gun now, a new breech-loader, a Christmas gift; he would own and shoot it for almost seventy years, through two new pairs of barrels and locks and one new stock, until all that remained of the original gun was the silver-inlaid trigger-guard with his and McCaslin's engraved names and the date in 1878. He found the tree beside the little bayou where he had stood that morning. Using the compass he ranged from that point; he was teaching himself to be better than a fair woodsman without even knowing he was doing it. On the third day he even found the gutted log where he had first seen the print. It was almost completely crumbled now, healing with unbelievable speed, a passionate and almost visible relinquishment, back into the earth from which the tree had grown. He ranged the summer woods now, green with gloom, if anything actually dimmer than they had been in November's grey dissolution, where even at noon the sun fell only in windless dappling upon the earth which never completely dried and which crawled with snakes—moccasins and water-snakes and rattlers, themselves the colour of the dappled gloom so that he would not always see them until they moved; returning to camp later and later, first day, second day, passing in the twilight of the third evening the little log pen enclosing the log barn where Sam was putting up the stock for the night. 'You aint looked right yet,' Sam said.

He stopped. For a moment he didn't answer. Then he said peacefully, in a peaceful rushing burst, as when a boy's miniature dam in a little brook gives way: 'All right. Yes. But how? I went to the bayou. I even found that log again. I—'

'I reckon that was all right. Likely he's been watching you. You never saw his foot?'

'I ...' the boy said. 'I didn't ... I never thought ...'

'It's the gun,' Sam said. He stood beside the fence, motionless, the old man, son of a negro slave and a Chickasaw

76

chief, in the battered and faded overall and the frayed five-cent straw hat which had been the badge of the negro's slavery and was not the regalia of his freedom. The camp—the clearing, the house, the barn and its tiny lot with which Major de Spain in his turn had scratched punily and evanescently at the wilderness—faded in the dusk, back into the immemorial darkness of the woods. *The gun*, the boy thought. *The gun*. 'You will have to choose,' Sam said.

He left the next morning before light, without breakfast, long before Uncle Ash would wake in his quilts on the kitchen floor and start the fire. He had only the compass and a stick for the snakes. He could go almost a mile before he would need to see the compass. He sat on a log, the invisible compass in his hand, while the secret night-sounds which had ceased at his movements, scurried again and then fell still for good and the owls ceased and gave over to the waking day birds and there was light in the grey wet woods and he could see the compass. He went fast yet still quietly, becoming steadily better and better as a woodsman without yet having time to realize it; he jumped a doe and a fawn, walked them out of the bed, close enough to see them—the crash of undergrowth, the white scut, the fawn scudding along behind her, faster than he had known it could have run. He was hunting right, upwind, as Sam had taught him, but that didn't matter now. He had left the gun; by his own will and relinquishment he had accepted not a gambit, not a choice, but a condition in which not only the bear's heretofore inviolable anonymity but all the ancient rules and balances of hunter and hunted had been abrogated. He would not even be afraid, not even in the moment when the fear would take him completely: blood, skin, bowels, bones, memory from the long time before it even became his memory—all save that thin clear quenchless lucidity which alone differed him from this bear and from all the other bears and bucks he would follow during almost seventy years, to which Sam had said: 'Be scared. You cant help that. But dont be afraid. Aint nothing in the woods going

77

to hurt you if you dont corner it or it dont smell that you are afraid. A bear or a deer has got to be scared of a coward the same as a brave man has got to be.'

By noon he was far beyond the crossing on the little bayou, farther into the new and alien country than he had ever been, travelling now not only by the compass but by the old, heavy, biscuit-thick silver watch which had been his father's. He had left the camp nine hours ago; nine hours from now, dark would already have been an hour old. He stopped, for the first time since he had risen from the log when he could see the compass face at last, and looked about, mopping his sweating face on his sleeve. He had already relinquished, of his will, because of his need, in humility and peace and without regret, yet apparently that had not been enough, the leaving of the gun was not enough. He stood for a moment—a child, alien and lost in the green and soaring gloom of the markless wilderness. Then he relinquished completely to it. It was the watch and the compass. He was still tainted. He removed the linked chain of the one and the looped thong of the other from his overall and hung them on a bush and leaned the stick beside them and entered it.

When he realized he was lost, he did as Sam had coached and drilled him: made a cast to cross his back-track. He had not been going very fast for the last two or three hours, and he had gone even less fast since he left the compass and watch on the bush. So he went slower still now, since the tree could not be very far; in fact, he found it before he really expected to and turned and went to it. But there was no bush beneath it, no compass nor watch, so he did next as Sam had coached and drilled him: made this next circle in the opposite direction and much larger, so that the pattern of the two of them would bisect his track somewhere, but crossing no trace nor mark anywhere of his feet or any feet, and now he was going faster though still not panicked, his heart beating a little more rapidly but strong and steady enough, and this time it was not even the tree because there was a down log beside it which he had never seen before and beyond the log a little swamp, a seepage of moisture somewhere between earth and water, and he did what Sam had coached and drilled him as the next and the last, seeing as he sat down on the log the crooked print, the warped indentation in the wet ground which while he looked at it continued to fill with water until it was level full and the water began to over-flow and the sides of the print began to dissolve away. Even as he looked up he saw the next one, and, moving, the one beyond it, moving, not hurrying, running, but merely keeping pace with them as they appeared before him as though they were being shaped out of thin air just one constant pace short of where he would lose them for ever and be lost for ever himself, tireless, eager, with-out doubt or dread, panting a little above the strong rapid little hammer of his heart, emerging suddenly into a little glade and the wilderness coalesced. It rushed, soundless, and solidified—the trees, the bush, the compass and the watch glinting where a ray of sunlight touched them. Then he saw the bear. It did not emerge, appear: it was just there, immobile, fixed in the green and windless noon's hot dappling, not as big as he had dreamed it but as big as he had expected, bigger, dimensionless against the dappled obscurity, looking at him. Then it moved. It crossed the glade without haste, walking for an instant into the sun's full glare and out of it, and stopped again and looked back at him across one shoulder. Then it was gone. It didn't walk into the woods. It faded, sank back into the wilderness without motion as he had watched a fish, a huge old bass, sink back into the dark depths of its pool and vanish without even any movement of its fins.

III

'But not enough. Not enough for even Father and Uncle Buddy to fumble-heed in even three generations not even three generations fathered by Grandfather not even if there had been nowhere beneath His sight any but Grandfather and so He would not even have needed to elect and choose.

79

But He tried and I know what you will say. That having Himself created them He could have known no more of hope than He could have pride and grief but He didn't hope He just waited because He had made them : not just because He had set them alive and in motion but because He had already worried with them so long; worried with them so long because He had seen how in individual cases they were capable of anything any height or depth remembered in mazed incomprehension out of heaven where hell was created too and so He must admit them or else admit His equal somewhere and so be no longer God and therefore must accept responsibility for what He Himself had done in order to live with Himself in His lonely and paramount heaven. And He probably knew it was vain but He had created them and knew them capable of all things because He had shaped them out of the primal Absolute which contained all and had watched them since in their individual exaltation and baseness and they themselves not knowing why nor how nor even when : until at last He saw that they were all Grandfather all of them and that even from them the elected and chosen the best the very best He could expect (not hope mind : not hope) would be Bucks and Buddies and not even enough of them and in the third generation not even Bucks and Buddies but—' and McCaslin

'Ah :' and he

'Yes. If He could see Father and Uncle Buddy in Grandfather. He must have seen me too—an Isaac born into a later life than Abraham's and repudiating immolation : fatherless and therefore safe declining the altar because maybe this time the exasperated Hand might not supply the kid—' and McCaslin

'Escape :' and he

'All right. Escape—Until one day He said what you told Fonsiba's husband that afternoon here in this room : *This will do. This is enough* : not in exasperation or rage or even just sick to death as you were sick that day : just *This is enough* and looked about for one last time, for one time more since He had created them, upon this land this South for which He had done so much with woods for game and

streams for fish and deep rich soil for seed and lush springs
to sprout it and long summers to mature it and serene falls
to harvest it and short mild winters for men and animals
and saw no hope anywhere and looked beyond it where
hope should have been, where to East North and West lay
illimitable that whole hopeful continent dedicated as a
refuge and sanctuary of liberty and freedom from what
you called the old world's worthless evening and saw the
rich descendants of slavers, females of both sexes, to whom
the black they shrieked of was another specimen another
example like the Brazilian macaw brought home in a
cage by a traveller, passing resolutions about horror and
outrage in warm and air-proof halls: and the thundering
cannonade of politicians earning votes and the medicine-
shows of pulpiteers earning Chatauqua fees, to whom the
outrage and the injustice were as much abstractions as
Tariff or Silver or Immortality and who employed the
very shackles of its servitude and the sorry rags of its
regalia as they did the other beer and banners and mot-
toes redfire and brimstone and sleight-of-hand and musical
handsaws: and the whirling wheels which manufactured
for a profit the pristine replacements of the shackles and
shoddy garments as they wore out and spun the cotton and
made the gins which ginned it and the cars and ships which
hauled it, and the men who ran the wheels for that profit
and established and collected the taxes it was taxed with
and the rates for hauling it and the commissions for selling
it: and He could have repudiated them since they were
his creation now and for evermore throughout all their
generations until not only that old world from which He
had rescued them but this new one too which He had
revealed and led them to as a sanctuary and refuge were
become the same worthless tideless rock cooling in the last
crimson evening except that out of all that empty sound
and bootless fury one silence, among that loud and moiling
all of them just one simple enough to believe that horror
and outrage were first and last simply horror and outrage
and was crude enough to act upon that, illiterate and had
no words for talking or perhaps was just busy and had

no time to, one out of them all who did not bother Him with cajolery and adjuration then pleading then threat and had not even bothered to inform Him in advance what he was about so that a lesser than He might have even missed the simple act of lifting the long ancestral musket down from the deer-horns above the door, whereupon He said *My name is Brown too* and the other *So is mine* and He *Then mine or yours cant be because I am against it* and the other *So am I* and He triumphantly *Then where are you going with that gun?* and the other told him in one sentence one word and He: amazed: Who knew neither hope nor pride nor grief *But your Association, your Committee, your Officers. Where are your Minutes, your Parliamentary Procedures?* and the other *I aint against them. They are all right I reckon for them that have the time. I am just against the weak because they are niggers being held in bondage by the strong just because they are white.* So He turned once more to this land which He still intended to save because He had done so much for it—' and McCaslin

'What?' and he

'—to these people He was still committed to because they were His creations—' and McCaslin.

'Turned back to us? His face to us?' and he

'—whose wives and daughters at least made soups and jellies for them when they were sick and carried the trays through the mud and the winter too into the stinking cabins and sat in the stinking cabins and kept fires going until crises came and passed but that was not enough: and when they were very sick had them carried into the big house itself into the company room itself maybe and nursed them there which the white man would have done too for any other of his cattle that was sick but at least the man who hired one from a livery wouldn't have and still that was not enough: so that He said and not in grief either Who had made them and so could know no more of grief than He could of pride or hope: *Apparently they can learn nothing save through suffering, remember nothing save when underlined in blood—*'

The Hamlet (1940)

In this passage the Snopeses make their inauspicious entry into the saga, and Faulkner tells it with ironical humour and a full sense of the futility of trying to oppose such cunning vitality and absence of common conscience. Jody Varner is the clerk of his father, Will Varner's store, at Frenchman's Bend. It is his sister who will become Flem Snopes's wife. Faulkner's yarning manner is at its best here, unfolding the tale as if spinning it out to an entranced audience.

The son, Jody, was about thirty, a prime bulging man, slightly thyroidic, who was not only unmarried but who emanated a quality of invincible and inviolable bachelordom as some people are said to breathe out the odor of sanctity or spirituality. He was a big man, already promising a considerable belly in ten or twelve years, though as yet he still managed to postulate something of the trig and unattached cavalier. He wore, winter and summer (save that in the warm season he dispensed with the coat) and Sundays and week days, a glazed collarless white shirt fastened at the neck with a heavy gold collar-button beneath a suit of good black broadcloth. He put on the suit the day it arrived from the Jefferson tailor and wore it every day and in all weathers thereafter until he sold it to one of the family's Negro retainers, so that on almost any Sunday night one whole one or some part of one of his old suits could be met—and promptly recognised—walking the summer roads, and replaced it with the new succeeding one. In contrast to the unvarying overalls of the men he lived among he had an air not funereal exactly but ceremonial —this because of that quality of invincible bachelorhood which he possessed: so that, looking at him you saw, beyond the flabbiness and the obscuring bulk, the perennial and immortal Best Man, the apotheosis of the masculine Singular, just as you discern beneath the dropsical tissue of the '09 halfback the lean hard ghost which once carried a ball. He was the ninth of his parents' sixteen children. He managed the store of which his father was still titular owner and in which they dealt mostly in foreclosed mortgages, and the gin, and oversaw the scattered farm holdings which his father at first and later the two of them together had been acquiring during the last forty years.

One afternoon he was in the store, cutting lengths of plowline from a spool of new cotton rope and looping them in neat seamanlike bights onto a row of nails in the wall, when at a sound behind him he turned and saw, silhouetted by the open door, a man smaller than common, in a wide hat and a frock coat too large for him, standing with a curious planted stiffness. 'You Varner?' the man said, in a voice not harsh exactly, or not deliberately harsh so much as rusty from infrequent use.

'I'm one Varner,' Jody said, in his bland hard quite pleasant voice. 'What can I do for you?'

'My name is Snopes. I heard you got a farm to rent.'

'That so?' Varner said, already moving so as to bring the other's face into the light. 'Just where did you hear that?' Because the farm was a new one, which he and his father had acquired through a foreclosure sale not a week ago, and the man was a complete stranger. He had never even heard the name before.

The other did not answer. Now Varner could see his

84

face—a pair of eyes of a cold opaque gray between shaggy graying irascible brows and a short scrabble of iron-gray beard as tight and knotted as a sheep's coat. 'Where you been farming?' Varner said.

'West.' He did not speak shortly. He merely pronounced the one word with a complete inflectionless finality, as if he had closed a door behind himself.

'You mean Texas?'

'No.'

'I see. Just west of here. How much family you got?'

'Six.' Now there was no perceptible pause, nor was there any hurrying on into the next word. But there was something. Varner sensed it even before the lifeless voice seemed deliberately to compound the inconsistency: 'Boy and two girls. Wife and her sister.'

'That's just five.'

'Myself,' the dead voice said.

'A man dont usually count himself among his own field hands,' Varner said. 'Is it five or is it seven.'

'I can put six hands into the field.'

Now Varner's voice did not change either, still pleasant, still hard: 'I don't know as I will take on a tenant this year. It's already almost first of May. I figure I might work it myself, with day labor. If I work it at all this year.'

'I'll work that way,' the other said. Varner looked at him.

'Little anxious to get settled, aint you?' The other said nothing. Varner could not tell whether the man was looking at him or not. 'What rent were you aiming to pay?'

'What do you rent for?'

'Third and fourth,' Varner said. 'Furnish out of the store here. No cash.'

'I see. Furnish in six-bit dollars.'

'That's right,' Varner said pleasantly. Now he could not tell if the man were looking at anything at all or not.

'I'll take it,' he said.

Standing on the gallery of the store, above the half dozen overalled men sitting or squatting about it with pocket knives and slivers of wood, Varner watched his caller limp stiffly across the porch, looking neither right nor left, and descend and from among the tethered teams and saddled animals below the gallery choose a gaunt saddleless mule in a worn plow bridle with rope reins and lead it to the steps and mount awkwardly and stiffly and ride away, still without once looking to either side. 'To hear that ere foot, you'd think he weighed two hundred pounds,' one of them said. 'Who's he, Jody?'

Varner sucked his teeth and spat into the road. 'Name's Snopes,' he said.

'Snopes?' a second man said. 'Sho now. So that's him.' Now not only Varner but all the others looked at the speaker—a gaunt man in absolutely clean though faded and patched overalls and even freshly shaven, with a gentle, almost sad face until you unravelled what were actually two separate expressions—a temporary one of static peace and quiet overlaying a constant one of definite even though faint harriedness, and a sensitive mouth which had a quality of adolescent freshness and bloom until you realised that this could just as well be the result of a life-long abstinence from tobacco—the face of the breathing archetype and protagonist of all men who marry young and father only daughters and are themselves but the eldest daughter of their own wives. His name was Tull. 'He's the fellow that wintered his family in a old cotton-house on Ike McCaslin's place. The one that was mixed up in that burnt barn of a fellow named Harris over in Grenier County two years ago.'

'Huh?' Varner said. 'What's that? Burnt barn?'

'I never said he done it,' Tull said. 'I just said he was kind of involved in it after a fashion you might say.'

'How much involved in it?'

'Harris had him arrested into court.'

'I see,' Varner said. 'Just a pure case of mistaken identity. He just hired it done.'

'It wasn't proved,' Tull said, 'Leastways, if Harris ever found any proof afterward, it was too late then. Because he had done left the country. Then he turned up at McCaslin's last September. Him and his family worked by

86

the day, gathering for McCaslin, and McCaslin let them winter in a old cottonhouse he wasn't using. That's all I know. I aint repeating nothing.'

'I wouldn't,' Varner said. 'A man dont want to get the name of a idle gossip.' He stood above them with his broad bland face, in his dingy formal black-and-white—the glazed soiled white shirt and the bagging and uncared-for trousers —a costume at once ceremonial and negligee. He sucked his teeth briefly and noisily. 'Well well well,' he said. 'A barn burner. Well well well.'

That night he told his father about it at the supper table. With the exception of the rambling half-log half-sawn plank edifice known as Littlejohn's hotel, Will Varner's was the only house in the country with more than one storey. They had a cook too, not only the only Negro servant but the only servant of any sort in the whole district. They had had her for years yet Mrs. Varner still said and apparently believed that she could not be trusted even to boil water unsupervised. He told it that evening while his mother, a plump cheery bustling woman who had borne sixteen children and already outlived five of them and who still won prizes for preserving fruits and vegetables at the annual county fair, bustled back and forth between dining room and kitchen, and his sister, a soft ample girl with definite breasts even at thirteen and eyes like cloudy hothouse grapes and a full damp mouth always slightly open, sat at her place in a kind of sullen bemusement of rife young female flesh, apparently not even having to make any effort not to listen.

'You already contracted with him?' Will Varner said.

'I hadn't aimed to at all till Vernon Tull told me what he did. Now I figure I'll take the paper up there tomorrow and let him sign.'

'Then you can point out to him which house to burn too. Or are you going to leave that to him?'

'Sho,' Jody said. 'We'll discuss that too.' Then he said— and now all levity was gone from his voice, all poste and riposte of humor's light whimsy, tierce quarto and prime: 'All I got to do is find out for sho about that barn. But then it will be the same thing, whether he actually did it or not. All he'll need will be to find out all of a sudden at gathering time that I think he did it. Listen. Take a case like this.' He leaned forward now, over the table, bulging, protuberant, intense. The mother had bustled out, to the kitchen, where her brisk voice could be heard scolding cheerfully at the Negro cook. The daughter was not listening at all. 'Here's a piece of land that the folks that own it hadn't actually figured on getting nothing out of this late in the season. And here comes a man and rents it on shares that the last place he rented on a barn got burnt up. It dont matter whether he actually burnt that barn or not, though it will simplify matters if I can find out for sho he did. The main thing is, it burnt while he was there and the evidence was such that he felt called on to leave the country. So here he comes and rents this land we hadn't figured on nothing out of this year nohow and we furnish him outen the store all regular and proper. And he makes his crop and the landlord sells it all regular and has the cash waiting and the fellow comes in to get his share and the landlord says, "What's this I heard about you and that barn?" That's all. "What's this I just heard about you and that barn?"' They stared at one another —the slightly protuberant opaque eyes and the little hard blue ones. 'What will he say? What can he say except "All right. What do you aim to do?"'

'You'll lose his furnish bill at the store.'

'Sho. There aint no way of getting around that. But after all, a man that's making you a crop free gratis for nothing, at least you can afford to feed him while he's doing it.—Wait', he said. 'Hell fire, we wont even need to do that; I'll just let him find a couple of rotten shingles with a match laid across them on his doorstep the morning after he finishes laying-by and he'll know it's all up then and aint nothing left for him but to move on. That'll cut two months off the furnish bill and all we'll be out is hiring his crop gathered.' They stared at one another. To one of them it was already done, accomplished: he could actually see it; when he spoke it was out of a time still six months in the future: 'Hell fire, he'll have to! He cant fight it! He dont dare!'

'Hmph,' Will said. From the pocket of his unbuttoned vest he took a stained cob pipe and began to fill it. 'You better stay clear of them folks.'

'Sho now,' Jody said. He took a toothpick from the china receptacle on the table and sat back. 'Burning barns aint right. And a man that's got habits that way will just have to suffer the disadvantages of them.'

He did not go the next day nor the one after that either. But early in the afternoon of the third day, his roan saddle horse hitched and waiting at one of the gallery posts, he sat at the roll-top desk in the rear of the store, hunched, the black hat on the back of his head and one broad black-haired hand motionless and heavy as a ham of meat on the paper and the pen in the other tracing the words of the contract in his heavy deliberate sprawling script. An hour after that and five miles from the village, the contract blotted and folded neatly into his hip pocket, he was sitting the horse beside a halted buckboard in the road. It was battered with rough usage and caked with last winter's dried mud, it was drawn by a pair of shaggy ponies as wild and active-looking as mountain goats and almost as small. To the rear of it was attached a sheet-iron box the size and shape of a dog kennel and painted to resemble a house, in each painted window of which a painted woman's face simpered above a painted sewing machine, and Varner sat his horse and glared in shocked and outraged consternation at its occupant, who had just said pleasantly, 'Well, Jody, I hear you got a new tenant.'

'Hell fire!' Varner cried. 'Do you mean he set fire to another one? even after they caught him, he set fire to *another* one?'

'Well,' the man in the buckboard said, 'I dont know as I would go on record as saying he set ere a one of them afire. I would put it that they both taken fire while he was more or less associated with them. You might say that fire seems to follow him around, like dogs follows some folks.' He spoke in a pleasant, lazy, equable voice which you did not discern at once to be even more shrewd than humorous. This was Ratliff, the sewing-machine agent. He lived in Jefferson and he travelled the better part of four counties with his sturdy team and the painted dog kennel into which an actual machine neatly fitted. On successive days and two counties apart the splashed and battered buckboard and the strong mismatched team might be seen tethered in the nearest shade and Ratliff's bland affable ready face and his neat tieless blue shirt one of the squatting group at a crossroads store, or—and still squatting and still doing the talking apparently though actually doing a good deal more listening than anybody believed until after-ward—among the women surrounded by laden clotheslines and tubs and blackened wash pots beside springs and wells, or decorous in a splint chair on cabin galleries, pleasant, affable, courteous, anecdotal and impenetrable. He sold perhaps three machines a year, the rest of the time trading in land and livestock and second-hand farming tools and musical instruments or anything else which the owner did not want badly enough, retailing from house to house the news of his four counties with the ubiquity of a news-paper and carrying personal messages from mouth to mouth about weddings and funerals and the preserving of vegetables and fruit with the reliability of a postal service. He never forgot a name and he knew everyone, man mule and dog, within fifty miles. 'Just say it was following along behind the wagon when Snopes druv up to the house De Spain had give them, with the furniture piled into the wagon bed like he had druv up to the house they had been living in at Harris's or wherever it was and said "Get in here" and the cookstove and beds and chairs come out and got in by their selves. Careless and yet good too, tight, like they was used to moving and not having no big help at it. And Ab and that big one, Flem they call him—there was another one too, a little one; I remember seeing him once somewhere. He wasn't with them. Leastways he aint now. Maybe they forgot to tell him when to get outen the barn.—setting on the seat and them two hulking gals in the two chairs in the wagon bed and Miz Snopes and her

sister, the widow, setting on the stuff in the back like
nobody cared much whether they come along or not
either, including the furniture. And the wagon stops in
front of the house and Ab looks at it and says, "Likely
it aint fitten for hawgs." '

Sitting the horse, Varner glared down at Ratliff in protuberant and speechless horror. 'All right,' Ratliff said.
'Soon as the wagon stopped Miz Snopes and the widow got
out and commenced to unload. Them two gals aint moved
yet, just setting there in them two chairs, in their Sunday
clothes, chewing sweet gum, till Ab turned round and
cussed them outen the wagon to where Miz Snopes and
the widow was wrastling with the stove. He druv them
out like a pair of heifers just a little too valuable to hit
hard with a stick, and then him and Flem set there and
watched them two strapping gals take a wore-out broom
and a lantern outen the wagon and stand there again till
Ab leant out and snicked the nigh one across the stern
with the end of the reins. "And then you come back and
help your maw with that stove," he hollers after them.
Then him and Flem got outen the wagon and went up to
call on De Spain.'

'To the barn?' Verner cried. 'You mean they went right
straight and——'

'No no. That was later. The barn come later. Likely they
never knowed just where it was yet. The barn burnt all
regular and in due course; you'll have to say that for him.
This here was just a call, just pure friendship, because
Snopes knowed where his fields was and all he had to do
was to start scratching them, and it already the middle of
May. Just like now,' he added in a tone of absolutely cream-
like innocence. 'But then I hear tell he always makes his
rent contracts later than most.' But he was not laughing.
The shrewd brown face was as bland and smooth as ever
beneath the shrewd impenetrable eyes.

'Well?' Varner said violently. 'If he sets his fires like
you tell about, I reckon I dont need to worry until Christmas. Get on with it. What does he have to do before he
starts lighting matches? Maybe I can recognise at least

some of the symptoms in time.'

'All right,' Ratliff said. 'So they went up the road, leaving Miz Snopes and the widow wrastling at the cookstove and them two gals standing there now holding a wire rat-trap and a chamber pot, and went up to Major de Spain's and walked up the private road where that pile of fresh horse manure was and the nigger said Ab stepped in it on deliberate purpose. Maybe the nigger was watching them through the front window. Anyway Ab tracked it right across the front porch and knocked and when the nigger told him to wipe it offen his feet, Ab shoved right past the nigger and the nigger said he wiped the rest of it off right on that ere hundred-dollar rug and stood there hollering "Hello. Hello, De Spain" until Miz de Spain come and looked at the rug and at Ab and told him to please go away.'

The Mansion (1959)

The murder of Flem Snopes by his cousin Mink draws the Snopes saga to its conclusion. Faulkner compresses the family's history into the time it takes Mink to leave the truck in which a Negro has just given him a lift, make his way to Flem's house and aim. The energy of the prose stems from Faulkner's rapid succession of distance shots, close-ups, and slowing down and speeding up of time within the reflexive sense of the past encroaching at last on the present.

Then the truck was gone. The road was empty when he left it. Out of sight from the road would be far enough. Only, if possible, nobody must even hear the sound of the trial shot. He didn't know why; he could not have said that, having had to do without privacy for thirty-eight years, he now wanted, intended to savour, every minuscule of it which freedom entitled him to; also he still had five or six hours until dark, and probably even less than that many miles, following the dense brier-cypress-willow jungle of the creek bottom for perhaps a quarter of a mile, maybe more, when suddenly he stopped dead with a kind of amazed excitement, even exhilaration. Before him, spanning the creek was a railroad trestle. Now he not only knew how to reach Jefferson without the constant risk of passing the people who from that old Yoknapatawpha County affinity would know who he was and what he intended to do, he would have something to do to pass the time until dark when he could go on.

It was as though he had not seen a railroad in thirty-eight years. One ran along one entire flank of the Parchman wire and he could see trains on it as far as he recalled every day. Also, from time to time gangs of convicts under their shotgun guards did rough construction or repair public work jobs in sight of railroads through the Delta where he could see trains. But even without the intervening wire, he looked at them from prison; the trains themselves were looked at, seen, alien in freedom, fleeing, existing in liberty and hence unreal, chimaeras, apparitions, without past or future, not even going anywhere since their destinations could not exist for him : just in motion a second, an instant, then nowhere; they had not been. But now it would be different. He could watch them, himself in freedom, as they fled past in freedom, the two of them mutual, in a way even interdependent : it to do the fleeing in smoke and noise and motion, he to do the watching; remembering how thirty-eight or forty years ago, just before he went to Parchman in fact—this occasion connected also with some crisis in his affairs which he had forgotten now; but then so were all his moments : connected, involved in some crisis of the constant outrage and injustice he was always having to drop everything to cope with, handle, with no proper tools and equipment for it, not even the time to spare from the unremitting work it took to feed himself and his family; this was one of those moments or maybe it had been simply the desire to see the train which had brought him the twenty-two miles in from Frenchman's Bend. Anyway, he had had to pass the night in town whatever the reason was and had gone down to the depot to see the New Orleans-bound passenger train come in—the hissing engine, the lighted cars each with an uppity impudent nigger porter, one car in which people were eating supper while more niggers waited on them, before going back to the sleeping-cars that had actual beds in them; the train pausing for a moment then gone: a long airtight chunk of another world dragged along the dark earth for the poor folks in overalls like him to gape at free for a moment without the train itself, let alone the folks in it, even knowing he was there.

But as free to stand and watch it as any man even if he did wear overalls instead of diamonds; and as free now, until he remembered something else he had learned in Parchman during the long tedious years while he prepared for freedom—the information, the trivia he had had to accumulate since when the time, the freedom came, he might not know until too late when he lacked: there had not been a passenger train through Jefferson since 1935, that the railroad which old Colonel Sartoris (not the banker they called Colonel but his father, the real colonel, that had commanded all the local boys in the old slavery war) had built, which according to the old folks whom even he, Mink, knew and remembered, had been the biggest thing to happen in Yoknapatawpha County, that was to have linked Jefferson and all the county all the way from the Gulf of Mexico in one direction to the Great Lakes in the other, was now a fading weed-grown branch line knowing no wheels any more save two local freight trains more or less every day.

In which case, more than ever would the track, the right-of-way be his path into town where the privacy of freedom it had taken him thirty-eight years to earn would not be violated, so he turned and retraced his steps perhaps a hundred yards and stopped; there was nothing: only the dense jungle dappled with September-afternoon silence. He took out the pistol. *Hit does look like a cooter* he thought, with what at the moment he believed was just amusement, humour, until he realised it was despair because he knew now that the thing would not, could not possibly fire, so that when he adjusted the cylinder to bring the first of the three cartridges under the hammer and cocked it and aimed at the base of a cypress four or five feet away and pulled the trigger and heard the faint vacant click, his only emotion was calm vindication, almost of superiority, at having been right, of being in an unassailable position to say I told you so, not even remembering cocking the hammer again since this time he didn't know where the thing was aimed when it jerked and roared, incredible with muzzle-blast because of the short barrel; only now, almost too late, springing in one frantic convulsion to catch his hand back before it cocked and fired the pistol on the last remaining cartridge by simple reflex. But he caught himself in time, freeing thumb and finger completely from the pistol until he could reach across with his left hand and remove it from the right one which in another second might have left him with an empty and useless weapon after all this distance and care and time. *Maybe the last one won't shoot neither* he thought, but for only a moment, a second, less than a second, thinking *No sir. It will have to. It will jest have to. There ain't nothing else for it to do. I don't need to worry. Old Moster jest punishes; He don't play jokes.*

And now (it was barely two o'clock by the sun, at least four hours till sundown) he could even risk the ground once more, this late, this last time, especially as he had last night in the cotton truck on the credit side. So he moved on again, beneath and beyond the trestle this time, just in case somebody had heard the shot and came to look, and found a smooth place behind a log and lay down. At once he began to feel the slow, secret, tentative palping start as the old biding unimpatient unhurried ground said to itself, 'Well, well, be dawg if here ain't one already laying right here on my doorstep so to speak.' But it was all right, he could risk it for this short time.

It was almost as though he had an alarm clock; he woke exactly in time to see through a leafed interstice overhead the last of sun drain, fade from the zenith, just enough light left to find his way back through the jungle to the railroad and mount on to it. Though it was better here, enough of day left to see him most of the last mile to town before it faded completely, displaced by darkness random with the sparse lights of the town's purlieus, the beginning, the first quiet edge-of-town back street beneath the rigid semaphore arms of the crossing warning and a single lonely street light where the Negro boy on the bicycle had ample time to see him stand in the centre of the crossing and brake to a stop. 'Hidy, son,' he said, using the old country-Negroid idiom for 'live' too: 'Which-a-way from here does Mr Flem Snopes stay?'

By now, since the previous Thursday night in fact, from about nine-thirty or ten each night until daybreak the next morning, Flem Snopes had had a bodyguard, though no white person in Jefferson, including Snopes himself, except the guard's wife, knew it. His name was Luther Biglin, a countryman, a professional dog trainer and market hunter and farmer until the last sheriff's election. Not only was his wife the niece of the husband of Sheriff Ephriam Bishop's wife's sister. Biglin's mother was the sister of the rural political boss whose iron hand ruled one of the county divisions (as old Will Varner ruled his at French-man's Bend) which had elected Bishop sheriff. So Biglin was now jailor under Bishop's tenure. Though with a definite difference from the standard nepotic run. Where as often as not, the holders of such lesser hierarchic offices gave nothing to the position they encumbered, having not really wanted it anyway but accepting it merely under family pressure to keep some member of the opposite political faction out of it, Biglin brought to his the sort of passionate enthusiastic devotion and fidelity to the power and immaculacy and integrity of his kinsman-by-marriage's position as say Murat's orderly corporal might have felt toward the symbology of his master's baton.

He was not only honourable (even in his market hunting of venison and duck and quail, where he broke only the law: never his word), he was brave too. After Pearl Harbour, although his mother's brother might, probably could and would, have found or invented for him absolution from the draft, Biglin himself volunteered for the Marine Corps, finding to his amazement that by military standards he had next to no vision whatever in his right

97

eye. He had not noticed this himself. He was a radio man,
not a reading man, and in shooting (he was one of the
best wing shots in the county though in an exuberant
spendthrift southpaw fashion—he was left-handed, shooting from his left shoulder; in the course of two of his three
previous vocations he shot up more shells than anyone in
the county; at the age of thirty he had already shot out
two sets of shotgun barrels) the defect had been an actual
service to him since he had never had to train himself
to keep both eyes open and see the end of the gun and
target at the same instant, or half-close the right one to
eliminate parallax. So when (not by curiosity, but by
simple bureaucratic consanguinity) he learned—even
quicker than the Sheriff did because he, Biglin, immediately
believed it—that the Mink Snopes free at last from the
state penitentiary, his old threats against his cousin, even
though forty years old, durst not be ignored, let alone
dismissed as his patron and superior seemed inclined to do.

So his aim, intent, was still basically to defend and preserve the immaculacy of his kinsman-by-marriage's office,
which was to preserve the peace and protect human life
and well-being, in which he modestly shared. But there
was something else too, though only his wife knew it. Even
the Sheriff didn't know about his plan, campaign; he only
told his wife: 'There may be nothing to it, like Cousin Eef
says: just another of Lawyer Stevens's nightmares. But
suppose Cousin Eef is wrong and Lawyer is right; suppose—' He could visualise it: the last split second, Mr
Snopes helpless in bed beneath his doom, one last hopeless
cry for the help which he knew was not there, the knife
(hatchet, hammer, stick of stovewood, whatever the ven-
geance-ridden murderer would use) already desending when
he, Biglin, would step, crash in, flashlight in one hand and
pistol in the other: one single shot, the assassin falling
across his victim, the expression of demonic anticipation
and triumph fading to astonishment on his face—'Why,
Mr Snopes will make us rich! He'll have to! There won't
be nothing else he can do!'

Since Mr Snopes mustn't know about it either (the

Sheriff had explained to him that in America you can't wet-nurse a free man unless he requests it or at least knowingly accepts it), he could not be inside the bedroom itself, where he should be, but would have to take the best station he could find or contrive outside the nearest window he could enter fastest or at least see to aim through. Which meant of course he would have to sit up all night. He was a good jailor, conscientious, keeping his jail clean and his prisoners properly fed and tended; besides the errands he did for the Sheriff. Thus the only time he would have to sleep in during the twenty-four hours would be between supper and the latest imperative moment moment when he must be at his station outside Snopes's bedroom window. So each night he would go to bed immediately after he rose from the supper table, and his wife would go to the picture show, on her return from which, usually about nine-thirty, she would wake him. Then, with his flashlight and pistol and a sandwich and a folding chair and a sweater against the chill as the late September nights cooled toward midnight, he would stand motionless and silent against the hedge facing the window where, as all Jefferson knew, Snopes spent all his life outside the bank, until the light went out at last; by which time, the two Negro servants would have long since left. Then he would move quietly across the lawn and open the chair beneath the window and sit down, sitting so immobile that the stray dogs which roamed all Jefferson during the hours of darkness, would be almost upon him before they would sense, smell, however they did it, that he was not asleep, and crouch and whirl in one silent motion and flee; until first light, when he would fold up the chair and make sure the crumpled sandwich wrapping was in his pocket, and depart; though by Sunday night, if Snopes had not been asleep and his daughter was not stone deaf, now and then they could have heard him snoring—until, that is, the nocturnal dog crossing the lawn this time would tense, smell—however they did it—that he was asleep and harmless until actually touched by the cold nose.

Mink didn't know that. But even if he had, it probably would have made little difference. He would simply have regarded the whole thing—Biglin, the fact that Snopes was now being guarded—as just one more symptom of the infinite capacity for petty invention of the inimical forces which had always dogged his life. So even if he had known that Biglin was already on station under the window of the room where his cousin now sat (He had not hurried. On the contrary: once the Negro boy on the bicycle had given him directions, he thought *I'm even a little ahead. Let them eat supper first and give them two niggers time to be outen the way.*) he would have behaved no differently: not hiding, not lurking: just unseen unheard and irrevocably alien like a coyote or a small wolf; not crouching, not concealed by the hedge as Biglin himself would do when he arrived, but simply squatting on his hams—as, a countryman, he could do for hours without discomfort—against it while he examined the house whose shape and setting he already knew out of the slow infinitesimal Parchman trickle of facts and information which he had had to garner, assimilate, from strangers yet still conceal from them the import of what he asked; looking in fact at the vast white columned edifice with something like pride that someone named Snopes owned it; a complete and absolute unjealousy: at another time, tomorrow, though he himself would never dream nor really ever want to be received in it, he would have said proudly to a stranger: 'My cousin lives there. He owns it.'

It looked exactly as he had known it would. There were the lighted rear windows of the corner room where his cousin would be sitting (they would surely have finished supper by now; he had given them plenty of time) with his feet propped on the little special ledge he had heard in Parchman how another kinsman Mink had never seen, Wat Snopes having been born too late, had nailed on to the hearth for that purpose. There were lights also in the windows of the room in front of that one, which he had not expected, knowing also about the special room upstairs the deaf daughter had fixed up for herself. But no light showed upstairs at all, so evidently the daughter was still downstairs too. And although the lights in the kitchen indicated that the two Negro servants had not left either, his impulse was so strong that he had already begun to rise without waiting longer, to cross to the window and see, if necessary begin now; who had thirty-eight years to practise patience in and should have been perfect. Because if he waited too long, his cousin might be in bed, perhaps even asleep. Which would be intolerable and must not be: there must be that moment, even if it lasted only a second, for him to say, 'Look at me, Flem,' and his cousin would do so. But he restrained himself, who had had thirty-eight years to learn to wait in, and sank, squatted back again, easing the hard lump of the pistol which he now carried inside the bib front of his overalls; her room would be on the other side of the house where he couldn't see the lighted windows from here, and the lights in the other room meant nothing since if he was big rich like his cousin Flem, with a fine big house like that, he would have all the lights on downstairs too.

Then the lights went off in the kitchen; presently he could hear the Negro man and the woman still talking as they approached and (he didn't even hold his breath) passed within ten feet of him and went through the gate in the hedge, the voices moving slowly up the lane beyond it until they died away. Then he rose, quietly, without haste, not furtive, not slinking: just small, just colourless, perhaps simply too small to be noticed, and crossed the lawn to the window and (he had to stand on tiptoe) looked into it at his cousin sitting in the swivel chair like in a bank or an office, with his feet propped against the chimney and his hat on, as he, Mink, had known he would be sitting, looking not too different even though Mink hadn't seen him in forty years; a little changed of course: the black planter's hat he had heard about in Parchman but the little bow tie might have been the same one he had been wearing forty years ago behind the counter in Varner's store, the shirt a white city shirt and the pants dark city pants too and the shoes polished city shoes instead of farmer's brogans. But no different, really: not reading, just sitting there with his feet propped and his hat on, his jaw moving faintly and steadily as if he were chewing.

Just to be sure, he would circle the house until he could see the lighted upper windows on the other side and had already started around the back when he thought how he might as well look into the other lighted room also while he was this close to it and moved, no less quiet than a shadow and with not much more substance, along the wall until he could stand on tiptoe again and look in the next window, the next room. He saw her at once and knew her at once—a room walled almost to the ceiling with more books than he knew existed, a woman sitting beneath a lamp in the middle of the room reading one, in horn-rim glasses and that single white streak through the centre of her black hair that he had heard about in Parchman too. For a second the old helpless fury and outrage possessed him again and almost ruined, destroyed him this time— the rage and fury when, during the first two or three years after he learned that she was back home again apparently for good and living right there in the house with Flem, he would think *Suppose she ain't deaf a-tall; suppose she's jest simply got every body fooled for whatever devilment of her own she's up to* since this—the real truth of whether she was deaf or just pretending—was one gambit which he would not only have to depend on somebody else for, but on something as frail and undependable as second- or third-hand hearsay. Finally he had lied, tricked his way in to the prison doctor but there he was again: daring not to ask what he wanted to know, had to know, find out, learn: only that even the stone-deaf would—could—feel the concussion of the air if the sound were loud enough or close enough. 'Like a—' Mink said before he could stop himself. But too late; the doctor finished it for him: 'That's right. A shot. But even if you could make us believe you are, how would that get you out of here?' 'That's right,' Mink said. 'I wouldn't need to hear that bull whip: jest feel it.'

But that would be all right; there was that room she had

fixed up for herself upstairs, while every word from home
that trickled down to him in Parchman—you had to believe folks sometimes, you had to, you jest had to—told
how his cousin spent all his time in the one downstairs
cattycorner across that house that was bigger they said than
even the jail. Then to look in the window and find her,
not upstairs and across the house where she should have
been, where in a way it had been promised to him she
would be, but right there in the next room. In which case
everything else he had believed in and depended on until
now was probably trash and rubble too; there didn't even
need to be an open door between the two rooms so she
could be sure to feel what the prison doctor had called
the concussion because she wasn't even deaf. Everything
had lied to him; he thought quietly *And I aint even got but
one bullet left even if I would have time to use two before
somebody come busting in from the street. I got to find a
stick of stovewood or a piece of ahrn somewhere*—that
close, that near to ruination and destruction before he
caught himself back right on the brink, murmuring, whispering, 'Wait now, wait. Ain't I told you and told you
Old Moster don't play jokes; He jest punishes? Of course
she's deaf: ain't all up and down Missippi been telling you
that for ten years now? I don't mean that durn Parchman
doctor nor all the rest of them durn jailbird son of a
bitches that was all I had to try to find out what I had
to know from, but that nigger jest yestiddy evening that
got almost impident, durn nigh called a white man a liar
to his face the least suh-jestion I made that maybe she was
fooling folks. Niggers that don't only know all the under-
cover about white folks, let alone one that they already
claim is a nigger lover and even one of the commonists to
boot, until all the niggers in Yoknapatawpha County and
likely Memphis and Chicago too know the truth about
whether she is deaf or not or ever thing else about her or
not. Of course she's deaf, setting there with her back
already to the door where you got to pass and they's
bound to be a back door too that all you got to do is
jest find it and walk right on out.' and moved on, without

haste: not furtive, just small and light-footed and invisible, on around the house and up the steps and on between the soaring columns of the portico like any other guest, visitor, caller, opening the screen door quietly into the hall and through it, passing the open door beyond which the woman sat, not even glancing toward it, and went on to the next one and drew the pistol from his overall bib; and, thinking hurriedly, a little chaotically, almost like tiny panting *I ain't got but one bullet so it will have to be in the face, the head; I can't resk jest the body with jest one bullet* entered the room where his cousin sat and ran a few more steps towards him.

He didn't need to say, 'Look at me, Flem.' His cousin was already doing that, his head turned over his shoulder. Otherwise he hadn't moved, only the jaws ceased chewing in midmotion. Then he moved, leaned slightly forward in the chair and he had just begun to lower his propped feet from the ledge, the chair beginning to swivel around, when Mink from about five feet away stopped and raised the toad-shaped iron-rust-coloured weapon in both hands and cocked and steadied it thinking *Hit's got to hit his face:* not *I've got to* but *It's got to* and pulled the trigger and rather felt than heard the dull foolish almost inattentive click. Now his cousin, his feet now flat on the floor and the chair almost swivelled to face him, appeared to sit immobile and even detached too, watching too Mink's grimed shaking child-size hands like the hands of a pet coon as one of them lifted the hammer enough for the other to roll the cylinder back one notch so that the shell would come again under the hammer; again that faint something out of the past nudged, prodded: not a warning nor even really a repetition: just faint and familiar and unimportant still since, whatever it had been, even before it had not been strong enough to be remembered; in the same second he had dismissed it. *Hit's all right* he thought *Hit'll go this time: Old Moster don't play jokes* and cocked and steadied the pistol again in both hands, his cousin not moving at all now though he was chewing faintly again, as though he too were watching the dull point of light on the cock of the hammer when it flicked away.

It made a tremendous sound though in the same instant Mink no longer heard it. His cousin's body was now making a curious half-stifled convulsive surge which in another moment was going to carry the whole chair over; it seemed to him, Mink, that the report of the pistol was nothing but that when the chair finished falling and crashed to the floor, the sound would wake all Jefferson. He whirled; there was a moment yet when he tried to say, cry, 'Stop! Stop! You got to make sho he's dead or you will have throwed away ever thing!' but he could not, he didn't remember when he had noticed the other door in the wall beyond the chair but it was there; where it led to didn't matter just so it led on and not back. He ran to it, scrabbling at the knob, still shaking the knob, quite blind now, even after the voice spoke behind him and he whirled again and saw the woman standing in the hall door; for an instant he thought *So she could hear all the time* before he knew better: she didn't need to hear; it was the same power had brought her here to catch him that by merely pointing her finger at him could blast, annihilate, vaporise him where he stood. And no time to cock and aim the pistol again even if he had had another bullet so even as he whirled he flung, threw the pistol at her, nor even able to follow that because in the same second it seemed to him she already had the pistol in her hand, holding it toward him, saying in that quacking duck's voice that deaf people use:

'Here: Come and take it. That door is a closet. You'll have to come back this way to get out.'

Bibliography

1 *The Works of William Faulkner*
(*in chronological order of publication*)

The Marble Faun, 1924 (poems).
Soldiers' Pay, 1926 (novel).
Mosquitoes, 1927 (novel).
Sartoris, 1929 (novel).
The Sound and the Fury, 1929 (novel).
As I Lay Dying, 1930 (novel).
Sanctuary, 1931 (novel).
These 13, 1931 (short stories).
Idyll in the Desert, 1931 (short story).
Miss Zilphia Grant, 1932 (short story).
Light in August, 1932 (novel).
A Green Bough, 1933 (poems).
Doctor Martino and Other Stories, 1934 (short stories).
Pylon, 1935 (novel).
Absalom, Absalom, 1936 (novel).
The Unvanquished, 1938 (novel of seven stories).
The Wild Palms, 1939 (novel).
The Hamlet, 1940 (novel).
Go Down, Moses, 1942 (novel of seven stories).
Intruder in the Dust, 1948 (novel).

Knight's Gambit, 1949 (short stories).
Collected Short Stories of William Faulkner, 1950.
Notes on a Horsethief, 1951 (episode later incorporated into *A Fable*).
Requiem for a Nun, 1951 (novel).
A Fable, 1954 (novel).
The Town, 1957 (novel).
The Mansion, 1959 (novel).
The Reivers, 1962 (novel).

2 *Conversations, Interviews, Anthologies, Letters*

ROBERT A. JELLIFFE (ed.), *Faulkner at Nagano*, Tokyo, 1956.
MALCOLM COWLEY (ed.), *Writers At Work: The Paris Review Interviews*, New York, 1958. (Contains a 1956 interview with Faulkner).
FREDERICK L. GWYNNE and JOSEPH L. BLOTNER (ed.), *Faulkner in the University*, University of Virginia, 1959.
JOSEPH L. FANT and ROBERT ASHLEY (ed.), *Faulkner at West Point*, New York, 1964.
JAMES B. MERIWETHER (ed.), *Essays, Speeches and Public Letters*, New York, 1966.
MALCOLM COWLEY (ed.), *The Faulkner-Cowley File: Letters and Memories 1944-1962*, New York, 1966.
MALCOLM COWLEY (ed.), *The Portable Faulkner*, New York, 1946; revised edition, 1966. (A pioneering anthology of stories and episodes from the novels linked by an introduction, notes and an appendix to make 'organic unity' out of Faulkner's Yoknapatawpha fictions.)
JAMES B. MERIWETHER and MICHAEL MILLGATE (ed.), *Lion in the Garden: Interviews with William Faulkner, 1926-1962*, New York, 1968. (Contains *Faulkner at Nagano* in its three hundred pages.)

3 *Bibliographical Materials*

JAMES B. MERIWETHER, *William Faulkner: A Check List*, 1957.

BIBLIOGRAPHY

JAMES B. MERIWETHER, *The Literary Career of William Faulkner: A Bibliographical Study*, 1961.

JAMES B. MERIWETHER, 'The Text of Faulkner's Books: an introduction and some notes', *Modern Fiction Studies*, IX, Summer 1963.

MAURICE BEEBE, 'Criticism of William Faulkner: A Selected Checklist', *Modern Fiction Studies*, XIII, Spring 1967.

4 *Critical and Biographical Works on William Faulkner*

MELVIN BACKMAN, *Faulkner: The Major Years—A Critical Study*, Indiana University Press, Bloomington and London, 1966. (A short, first-rate study of ten works between *Sartoris* and *Go Down, Moses*.)

CLEANTH BROOKS, *William Faulkner: The Yoknapatawpha County*, Yale University Press, New Haven and London, 1963. (The long first part of a two-volume study which relates the fiction to North Mississippi, considers all the works non-chronologically, and includes six family genealogies and a character index.)

MARGARET P. FORD and SUZANNE KINCAID, *Who's Who in Faulkner*, Louisiana State University Press, 1963. (Mainly a character index of key people in Faulkner's work, justified by his remark to students at the University of Virginia in 1957: 'I remember the people, but I can't remember what story they're in nor always what they did. I have to go back and look at it to unravel what the person was doing. I remember the character though'.)

IRVING HOWE, *William Faulkner: A Critical Study*, Vintage Books, Random House, New York, 1962, second edition. (A thorough account of Faulkner's world and a critical estimate of his achievement.)

FREDERICK J. HOFFMAN and OLGA W. VICKERY (ed.), *William Faulkner: Two Decades of Criticism*, Michigan, 1951. (Includes essays by Sartre, Cowley and many others.)

MICHAEL MILLGATE, *William Faulkner*, Oliver & Boyd, Edinburgh and London, 1961. (A useful short chronological account of the life and work in its Southern context, with a chapter on the critics.)

MICHAEL MILLGATE, *The Achievement of William Faulkner*, Constable, London, 1966. (Between a chapter of biography and a critical summary, there are nineteen chapters analysing the novels and one on the stories. A painstaking major study.)

WARD L. MINER, *The World of William Faulkner*, Duke University Press, 1952. (A short early study, still valuable for its comparison of fiction and actuality on the South, with an appendix of population figures for 1840-1950 in Lafayette County, Mississippi.)

Modern Fiction Studies Vol. XIII, No. 1, Spring 1967: William Faulkner Special Number, Purdue University, Indiana.

CHARLES H. NILON, *Faulkner and the Negro*, Citadel Press, New York, 1965. (An analysis of Faulkner's treatment of black characters; a detailed paraphrasing work which shows his destruction of the stereotype.)

PETER SWIGGART, *The Art of Faulkner's Novels*, University of Texas Press, Austin, 1962.

DOROTHY TUCK, *A Handbook of Faulkner*, Chatto & Windus, London, 1965. (Synopses, critical analyses, précis of stories, a history of Yoknapatawpha County, character biographies, genealogies, a biography of Faulkner, and a selected bibliography.)

ROBERT PENN WARREN (ed.), *Faulkner: A Collection of Critical Essays*, The Twentieth Century Views series, Prentice-Hall, New Jersey, 1966.

WILLIAM VAN O'CONNOR, *William Faulkner*, University of Minnesota Pamphlets on American Literature, 1959; reprinted in *Seven Modern American Novelists*, Minneapolis, 1964.

5 Supplementary Studies

W. J. CASH, *The Mind of the South*, New York, 1941. (An

BIBLIOGRAPHY

outstanding historical description of the culture of the South; a standard work.)

MARTIN J. DAIN, *Faulkner's County Yoknapatawpha*, Random House, New York, 1964. (A photographic essay which will provide a good visual image of Mississippi.)

JOHN M. BRADBURY, *Renaissance in the South: A Critical History of the Literature 1920-1960*, University of North Carolina Press/Oxford University Press, London, 1964. (Places Faulkner in the context of the literary culture of the South.)